AF687382

Mistnet Datamatics Morphotaxis for Synthoids

Polaris

Mistnet Datamatics Morphotaxis for Synthoids

First Edition September 2025

Written by Polaris

Contents

Chapter 7

Cloud-Enabled Robotic Framework using Landmark and Variable Length String

List of Figures

List of Tables

List of Abbreviations

Abbreviation	
API	Application Programming Interface
CPU	Central Processing Unit
GSM	Global System for Mobile communications
HFS	Hadoop File System
IOT	Internet of Things
jvm	Java Virtual Machine
KIF	Knowledge Interchange Format
M2C	Machine-to-Cloud
M2M	Machine-to-Machine
NFS	Network File System
PR2	Personal Robot
REST	Representational State Transfer
ROS	Robot Operating System
Wi-Fi	Wireless Fidelity
IR	Infra Red
LED	Light Emitting Diode

Chapter 1
Introduction

1.1 Background

Robotics as an academic entity is comparatively young with intensified goals of many directions; the ultimate is the creation of machines capable of acting and thinking like humans. Robots are machines, which are invented to replace or augment the jobs of humans [101]. The applications of robots in the real world are enormous [7, 101]. They are deployed in various scenarios where humans can be replaced mainly to do dangerous or tedious tasks under hazardous and hostile environments. The job may include from firefighting [38, 65, 110], deep sea or underwater [74, 69, 112, 119] to extreme space exploration [56, 70, 81, 106]. Robots could also be guided in a supermarket, art gallery, and hospitals or as a domestic helper [42, 101, 41] etc.

This crux of the problem of creating intelligent machines usually leads us to explore ourselves to know the mechanism of our bodies to function, the way they are viz., how limbs are coordinated, and how humans learn and perform complex tasks. This sense of questioning and imitating human beings is what makes robotics such a fascinating and engaging endeavor.

Some robots are autonomous [17], in the sense they work by themselves. Other robots need human intervention. Although robot has its origin dated back as early as the 13th century [27, 37], the word robot was coined in 1921 by "Karel Capek" in his play Rossum's Universal Robots (R.U.R) [10]. This word robot is derived from a Czech word, which means, "forced labor" [83]. Robots started gaining success in manufacturing industries in the 90s to automate applications throughout the production line saving time and money. Despite the success, they do have fundamental drawbacks in mobility since the robot arm or manipulator has a limited range of motion [101]. On the other hand with the introduction of 'mobile robots' [104], it could move from one part to another of a manufacturing plant [78]. A mobile robot traveling inside a known environment with a known obstacle becomes a problem when it is taken out outdoors in a real environment where the terrain is unknown to them [104]. Therefore, understanding robot parts becomes necessary to optimize or customize the robotic parts depending on the environment/condition in which they are deployed.

The main parts of a mobile robot consist of a Control system, Sensors, Actuators, Power supply and End effectors [47].

- ***Control System***: Human beings and other animals use feedback to survive in nature at the most basic level. They sense the environment to see what is going on around them and react accordingly. A robot's control system [46] also uses feedback just as the human or animal does. However, robots use a central processing unit, which is made up of silicon devices instead of a collection of neurons in human beings. Similar to what our brains decide what to do and how to react when we sense through our sensory organs, a robot's CPU does the same thing based on data collected by sensors attached to it.

- ***Sensors***: Sensors are devices that mimic human preceptor organs such as microphones that act as ears or cameras that function like eyes. A sensor senses the environment and gives feedback to the CPU of the robot. The robot's CPU in turn interprets these feedback signals and decides on its actions accordingly.

- ***Actuators***: They are motors which cause movement to any part of the robot. It is analogous to the muscle of a human being. It is similar to the action of human muscle to move parts of the human's body. Some robots may consist of few actuators for moving a particular part of the robot while advanced robots may have more actuators and may also be attached to wheels and threads for mobility.

- ***Power Supply***: Most of the industrial robots that are used in factories get their energy from electricity. Static robotics can be plugged in like any other appliance. Mobile robots are usually powered by batteries.

- ***End Effectors***: They are devices attached like human hand in robot to interact physically with the environment and to carry out tasks assigned to it.

1.2 Applications of Robots

Robots are meant to perform a variety of tasks in various fields. The amount of tasks delegated to robots is increasing. From the application point of view, the robots can be categorized in the following categories [7].

- **Industrial robots:** These robots help in applications such as- material handling, painting, welding etc. It can also consist of some automatically guided automobiles and other robots.

- **Domestic or household robots**: Robots which are used at home. This kind of robot does almost all the household chores like - robotic pool cleaners, robotic sweepers, robotic vacuum cleaners, robotic sewer cleaners etc.

- **Medical robots:** Robots that are used in medicine and medicinal institutes. They find extensive use in surgical treatment. Also, a number of robots direct automobiles and even help in lifting.

- **Service robots:** Robots that cannot be classified into any other types listed above but gives aid. These types of robots are used for collecting data, employed for research, etc.

- **Military robots:** Robots that are deployed in military and armed forces. These robots consist of bomb disposal robots, exploration and attacking drones etc.

- **Entertainment robots:** These types of robots are used for entertainment only.

- **Space robots:** This type of robots would consist of the robots employed in space. They are used for exploration in unknown environments or may be used for docking and fixing of space Shuttles by controlling from outside or for any other activities in space.

- **Hobby and competition robots:** These kinds of robots are created by students/children. It is made for fun, learning or for a certain contest.

The effects of automation technology are already felt in the entire economy [72]. In recent years, the global amount of industrial robots has grown quickly [49]. The dropping robots prices and the ability to function without disruption throughout the day, makes them cost-competitive with human employees. Computer algorithms in the service sector can run stock trades much more quickly in a fraction of a second than any other human being. As these techniques get cheaper [18], more capable and intelligent robots are finding its application in this economy driven environment.

Even as there are rapid significant advances in mobile robotics, the fundamental underlying limitations still remain the same, especially in the matter of power supply and efficient programs.

- **Power:** The limit or the range of mobile robots that can service depends on the power it draws from the onboard batteries. Therefore, it reduces the amount of tasks it could have completed. Recharging is sometimes not possible for autonomous robots, especially in places where charging points are difficult to locate. It also takes lots of time in processing huge and complicated data onboard the CPU of a robot thereby consuming much needed power [104].

- **Programs:** The cost of robots increases in the maintenance and repair of programs which drives the robots. In order to make robots smarter, the software needs to be updated to suit the changing requirements. Dealing with reinstallation of lost code or data may be time-consuming and sometimes costly. The robots cannot behave other than what they are programmed to do. In the current context due to availability of multiple platforms for mobile robots, the code written on a particular robot is not supported on other robots due to incompatibility of hardware. Therefore, it needs different programs/codes for each type of robot. It often requires a lot of re-coding as a result, increasing the cost and time of making robots.

The advent of the internet has changed the way programs/codes are written and executed, providing an enhanced mechanism for faster execution time with lesser resources. The

Internet has also enabled people to share and obtain information through the vast information stored in the World Wide Web (WWW) [64]. Distributed Computing has also eased the process of resources sharing such as memory and processing power of computers etc., mainly by pooling those resources from the participating computers. The cloud computing technology took a leap forward by facilitating devices to use storage and computing capability which are connected to the cloud [84]. As a result smaller and lighter devices with low power started depending on the cloud for their operations. Cloud provides processing power to these devices and thereby reducing the cost of processing power and decreased execution time [58]. These interventions lead to very highly energy efficient systems, which in turn became an advantage for the resources and power restricted mobile robots.

1.3 Cloud Computing

The term 'Cloud' is used for delivery of on-demand computing resources such as storage, software development platforms and servers over an internet from a remote server. Cloud Computing enables efficient use of resources sharing in various instances of computing in their remote distributed servers [122].

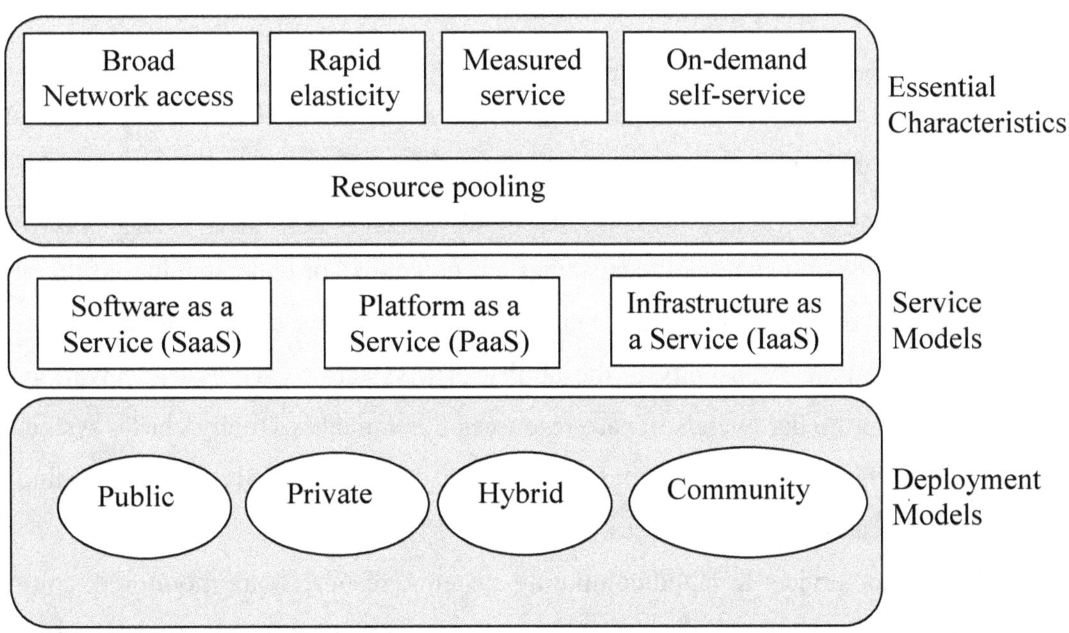

Figure 1.1 NIST's Definition of Cloud Computing [75].

As per the definition of NIST (National Institute of Standards and Technology, US Department of Commerce), "Cloud computing is a model for enabling ubiquitous, convenient, on-demand network access to a shared pool of configurable computing resources (e.g., networks, servers, storage, applications, and services) that can be rapidly provisioned and released with minimal management effort or service provider interaction" as shown in Figure 1.1 below [75].

As per the definition of NIST's cloud computing [75], the Cloud consists of five essential characteristics, three service models, and four deployment models, as stated below.

1.3.1 Essential Characteristics

On-demand self-service: A consumer uses the services of computing capabilities of cloud servers, such as server time and network storage etc. as and when needed automatically [75, 85].

a) Broad network access: It is the process of accessing the cloud computing server resources by heterogeneous thin or thick client such as a computer, net book, tablet computer, smart phone, or other devices.
b) Resource pooling: The computing resources from the cloud are pooled to facilitate different consumers using a multi-tenant model wherein the different physical and virtual resources are dynamically assigned and reassigned according to consumer's need [75, 89]. In general, the customer has no control or understanding of the precise place of the supplied resources, but can indicate a greater abstraction level.
c) Rapid elasticity: Elasticity is the ability of a system to increase the workload by increasing the hardware/software resources dynamically. Highly elastic systems can handle the increased demand and traffic by dynamically commissioning and decommissioning the resources. [71, 75].
d) Measured service: In cloud computing systems, resources are monitored, controlled and metered [75]. This enables consumers to pay for what is used or prepay for resource usage.

1.3.2 Service Models

The various types of services provided by the cloud can be broadly classified into the following three models.

a) Software as a Service (SaaS): The consumer is allowed to use the service of provider's applications running on a cloud infrastructure [60, 75]. Various devices through an interface can access these applications.

b) Platform as a Service (PaaS): The consumers can deploy the applications made by them or acquired applications created using programming languages and tools etc. supported by the Platform provider [57, 75]. However, the user may not have control over the operating system, network, storage etc.

c) Infrastructure as a Service (IaaS): In this case, the consumer can access fundamental computing resources such as storage, networks, processing etc. and can create fully functional instances of a system[59, 75]. The consumer can get their required storage, procession power etc. and run their system/application programs.

1.3.3 Deployment Models

The cloud can be either deployed privately or publicly as stated below.

a) Private cloud: This type of cloud infrastructure is usually deployed for a single entity or organization, which can be used by anyone of the organization [75]. It might be claimed, overseen, and worked by the association, an outsider, or some blend of them, and it might exist on or off premises.

b) Public cloud: This framework is for open use by the overall population. It might be possessed, overseen, and worked by a business, scholastic, or government association, or some blend of them [75]. It is situated at the premises of the cloud provider.

c) Hybrid cloud: Hybridization of the above three models by considering any two or all the three models can also be done. [75]

d) Community cloud: It is for the exclusive use by a specific community of consumers from organizations having the same area of concerns [75]. At least one of the networks in organizations, an outsider or some mixture can claim, oversee and operate it on the premises or outside it.

1.4 Cloud Robots

With the introduction of cloud computing, there has been a significant change in terms of computing and infrastructure management. Many enterprise's applications have successfully exploited the cloud computing approach [40, 102, 124] reducing their capital investment drastically. In terms of applications in robotics [50], the cloud infrastructure provides the much-needed heavy processing [48] and storage for its operation. It can also provide ways to interact and cooperate with many other robotic systems connected through the cloud. Since there are many applications and various kinds of tasks performed by robots, some of these tasks are done by using a group of robots working together [73].This team of robots can also use cloud for interaction and cooperation.

1.4.1 Cloud Robotic Service Models

By using the same paradigm of cloud computing, cloud robots can also have three robotic services for processing, storage and applications, as discussed below.

- Like IAAS, cloud robotics can also provide low-level resources, such as sensors and cameras at real time from different remote locations for sensing and recognition through the cloud. These capabilities can be seen with the introduction of the Internet *of Things (IOT)* [24, 51, 96, 114].
- Similar to PAAS, the robots connected through the cloud can have unlimited storage and computation resources. Any data such as a simple image, information about an obstacle or a plan etc. gathered by a robot, could be stored in the cloud [103]. This stored data can be used as a knowledge base available for sharing by other robots. Moreover, the robots can also use computational resources such as speech, image recognition etc. through the cloud [1, 9, 53, 55, 68].

- At a high level, like software as a service, platform independent, standard functions of robots can be used as a robot service. Heterogeneous robots should be able to execute these services irrespective of platform [8].

Hence, robots in conjunction with cloud computing technologies can have the following benefits.

- Cloud computing can provide on demand parallel computing for recognition, learning, and motion planning etc. By doing so, robots get lighter, smarter and cost effective.
- Robots can get access to vast resources of data that are not possible to maintain in onboard memory like databases of images, videos, maps and vast networks of sensors.
- The Cloud can facilitate sharing and exchanging of knowledge among heterogeneous robots with different hardware and software.

1.5 Limitations of Cloud Robotics

- The communication protocol used in the cloud is not secure [109]. It is constrained by its architectural design and deployment. Some of the challenges are also posed due to the characteristics like availability and reliability issues, data integrity, recovery, etc [34, 125]. It is also vulnerable to attacks as real time execution is required for robot-cloud communication.
- Low speed of the connection, device used for connection, network problem and high latency responses of cloud applications may make the robot brainless since the robot is dependent on the cloud.
- Two or more robots do not share the same platform and hence the program/code of one may not be compatible with the other [45]. Sharing and exchanging of knowledge among heterogeneous robots with different hardware and software may need a unified framework/platform which can be accepted universally by the robotics community.

1.6 Possible Solutions

The solutions to all the problems stated above, may not be possible to address exhaustively, but can be attempted to solve partially or logically. Since there are lots of parameters involved in securing a cloud computing environment [34, 61], it is not possible to find a security solution that fits all the constraints [31]. The vulnerabilities of cloud computing due to its deployment models, architecture, and its characteristics can be addressed using software engineering and information system design to some extent [100].

Bad network and high latency responses of cloud applications are an innate problem and cannot be solved. For slow speed, instead of exchanging huge data with the cloud, a universal light weight knowledge interchange format can be devised to follow as a standard command for robots. However in the case of deployment of multiple robots, the low speed device like Bluetooth etc. connected to the robots, can have a proxy based master robot with higher bandwidth [80].

Robots with different hardware and program code can be addressed at middleware or at higher level: In computing, middleware has enabled software developers to communicate operating systems with the applications by acting as an interface [22]. Similarly, a robotics middleware framework can give ease to developers for inter-operateability of heterogeneous robots under the cloud.

At a higher level, robots directly use the repository of Application Programming Interfaces (APIs) such as Google's speech recognition engine and Google vision API for object identifications [53].

1.7 Objectives

The main objectives of the thesis work are stated hereunder.

(i) To reduce redundant code and data for robots performing similar tasks by using the cloud enabled robotic framework for fixed length string communication.

(ii) To provide an interface between clouds and robots of different makes by using knowledge interchange format (KIF) and a variable length string.

(iii) To provide a suitable platform compatible to the robots under the cloud by introducing common representation for paths for the robot to navigate using natural landmarks in an unknown environment on cloud.

1.8 Organization of the Thesis

The thesis analyses the architectures and the features of several cloud robotics platforms for the development of a model to overcome some of the drawbacks in the existing model. The contributions of the thesis are organized as follows.

In Chapter 1, an introduction to robotics and the associated problems have been provided. It also includes various services provided by cloud computing, highlighting how robotics in conjunction with cloud computing can provide ways to interact and cooperate with many other robotic systems connected through it. It also gives a brief outline of various robotic service models.

Chapter 2 gives an overview of the related work in cloud robotics architecture. The drawbacks of the existing architecture are discussed. Also came up with possible solutions to the problems.

In Chapter 3, a generic architecture is proposed, wherein various cloud robotics services can be accommodated.

In chapter 4, a variable length string for the heterogeneous robots to communicate on the proposed architecture is discussed. The testing of proposed format in hadoop map-reduce is also discussed.

Chapter 5 is the Test bed 1 for testing the proposed architecture. It tests fixed length strings as data to be communicated between the robot and cloud. It also highlights the use of cloud to process Google's book database.

In Chapter 6, variable length string is used for testing the architecture as Test bed 2. It deals with the testing of heterogeneous robot communication with the proposed variable length string.

Chapter 7 introduces the generation of variable length string when the robot navigates in an unknown environment. It also demonstrates how navigation can be carried out through landmarks identified by Google's cloud vision.

Chapter 8 summarizes and concludes the work along with the limitations and future scope of the proposed work.

Chapter 2
Literature Survey

2.1 Background

In this era of fast growing technology, there exist a variety of robots of different makes with different types of hardware as well as the operational platforms. Since the robots generally do not have and/or share a common platform compatible for all types of hardware, a "write once fit all" code for the robots does not exist despite the advancement of technology. Hence, the concept of code reusability is almost non-existent. This is one of the main reasons why it is difficult to write software for robots and share the data when they are connected with the cloud. With the motive to simplify the task of creating complex and robust robot software behavior across different platforms, robots operating system (ROS) an open source framework was developed [55]. Motive of ROS was to meet the set of challenges that were encountered while developing service robots as part of projects like Stanford AI Robot (STAIR) and the Personal Robots (PR) program [92, 95]. ROS being open source has contributions from different communities with many new tools and libraries being updated. Despite these efforts the robotics communities are against the use of ROS [76, 105]. Reasons being, lack of support for some packages and availability of updates. Libraries are written and shared whenever there is a need for such libraries but failed to maintain bugs free, making them obsolete after a certain period of time. Still, the programs for robots are dependent highly on its hardware for its performance and function. Hence reusing of program code across varied platforms is difficult [88, 116]. The lack of standard interfaces [11, 19, 66, 96] for robot hardware components also continues to be a great challenge in all areas of robotics.

With a well-defined knowledge interchange format (KIF), ontology can be used to develop a new generation information system [12, 88].Thus it may help in merging and mapping of the information from different data source and preparing them in such a way that it can be made available to end users as a repository. The same concept can be deployed in the field of cloud robotics where robots can interact with each other and enables robots to share and reuse their existing information / knowledge [12, 19, 52].

Guoqiang Hu et al. [45] have proposed a cloud robotic architecture to improve the computation and information sharing capabilities of networked robotics. It consists of an ad-hoc cloud formed by machine-to-machine (M2M) communications among participating robots and an infrastructure cloud. Cloud robotics dynamically allocate the resources from a shared pool using a resilient computing model mainly to support task offloading and information sharing in robotic applications. Various communication protocols and elastic computing models have been proposed to handle different applications. The technicalities of computation, communication and security have also been discussed to highlight the potential benefits of cloud robotics in different applications [4].

Over the years, researchers have come up with different cloud robotics system architecture, the communication protocols and the language they used to communicate between cloud and the robots. Some of the notable architectures are presented in this section.

2.2 Cloud Platform

Waibel, et.al [115] for their work RoboEarth as shown in Figure 2.1 has developed a database where robots can interact with each other and the environment with the vision of forming a world wide web for robots. RoboEarth language comprises a semantic representation language for actions, objects, environments and the infrastructure to check the applicability of information in a given context and all the required capabilities of a robot [19]. Although data seems to be fundamental to robot learning and its extended performance beyond pre programmed tasks, more information does not translate into better performance automatically [99]. Rapyuta is an open source cloud robotics platform, which allows easy access to RoboEarth repository.

The robots that are connected to the Rapyuta have a system level clone that are highly interconnected on the cloud giving them the ability to offload heavy computation into the cloud [80], it provides a cloud infrastructure for building scalable cloud robotics applications. Rapyuta's computing environments are private, secure, and optimized for data throughput. However, its performance is in large part determined by the latency and quality of the network connection and the performance of the data center [80].

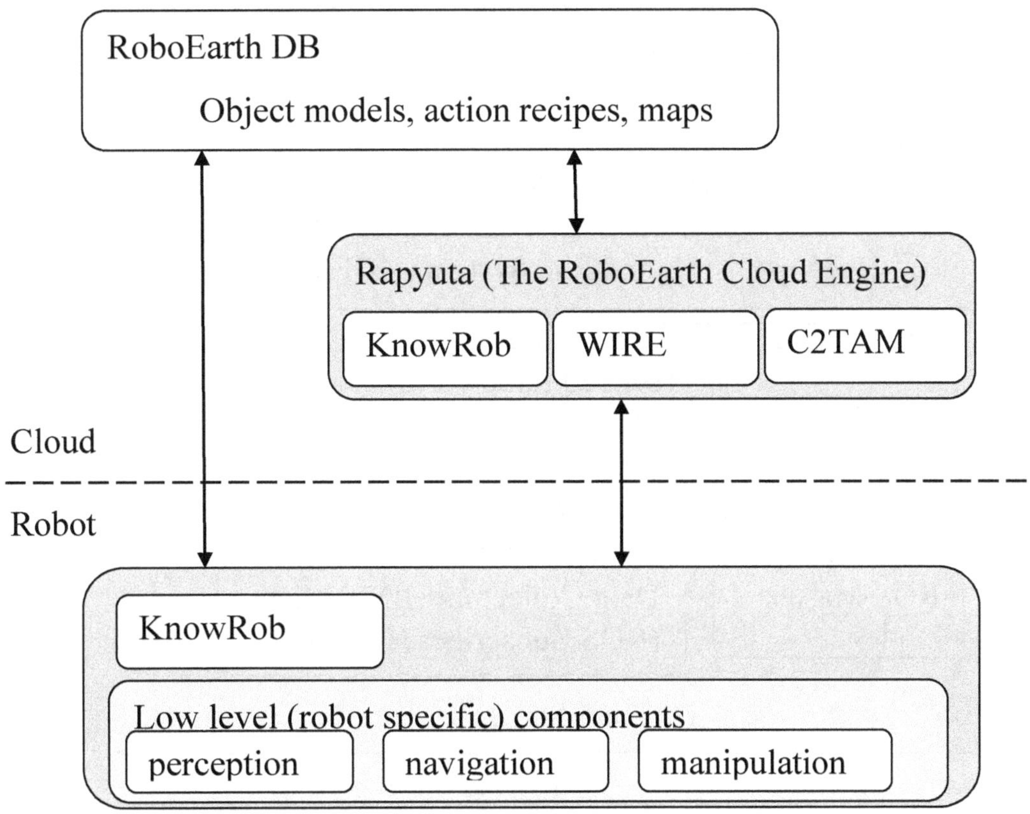

Figure 2.1 The RoboEarth System Architecture [115].

As shown in Figure 2.2, Davinci is a software framework that combines the distributed ROS architecture for data collection, the open source Hadoop Distributed File System (HDFS) for data storage and Hadoop Map Reduce Framework for batch processing of collected data providing the scalability and parallelism advantages of cloud computing for service Robots [53]. For communication with the Robots ROS is used. MapReduce includes a large number of disk seeks. The disk access significantly slows down the process thereby becoming the bottle-neck of this technique; Davinci framework did not consider this problem in their implementation [115].

2.3 Use of cloud

Rapyuta is used as an efficient infrastructure for making a scalable cloud robotics service for mapping and localization where low cost robots with RGB-D (red, blue, green and depth) sensors and smart class processors are used to run dense visual odometry algorithms [54,118]. Only the compressed key frames are sent to the cloud while the map optimization and merging are being done parallel in a commercial data center [90].

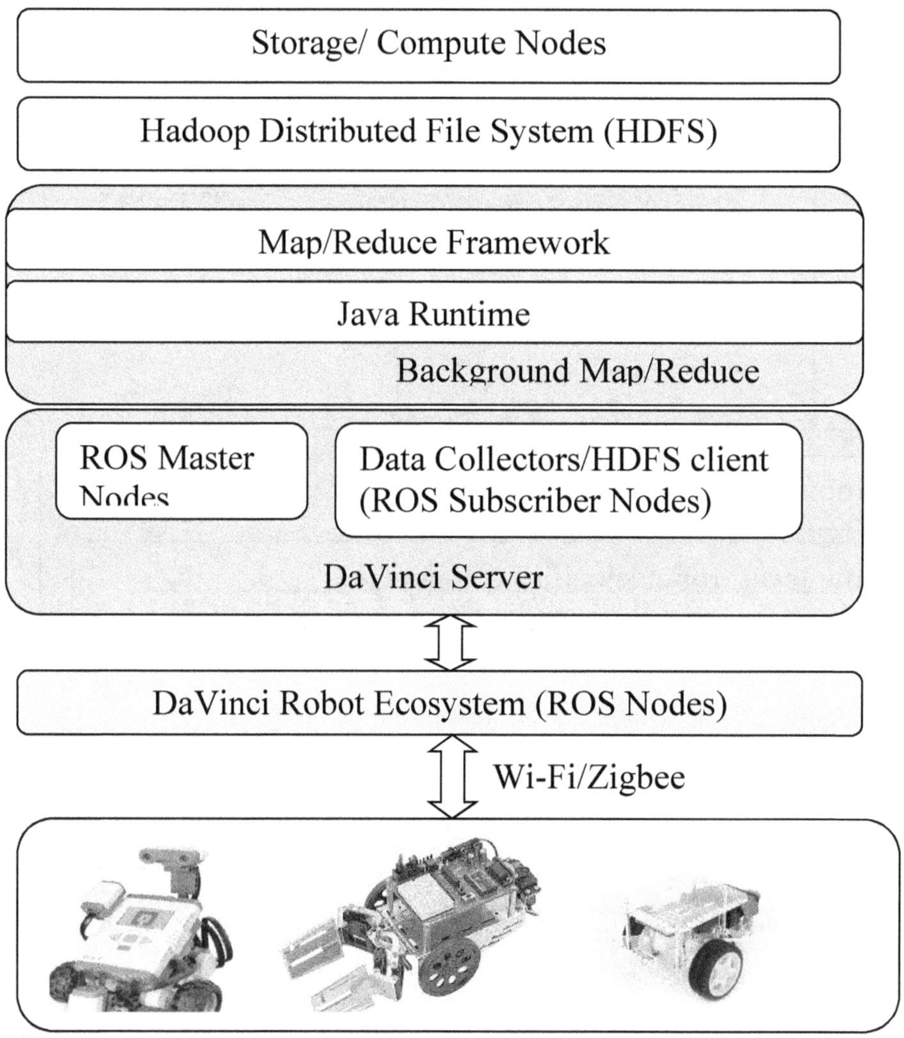

Figure 2.2 Architecture of Davinci Cloud Computing Platforms [3].

A distributed framework such as Simultaneous Localization and Mapping (SLAM) system is allocated as a service in the Cloud for the map optimization and storage that requires a lot of onboard computation. By using an Internet connection a lot of expensive onboard computation is reduced. Riazuelo et.al [90] has discussed the Real time performance of single Robot and cooperative SLAM, wherein a map database is used such that the maps can be built, stored, updated and shared. Kehoe et.al [53] has presented a Cloud-based robot grasping with the Google object recognition engine for recognizing and grasping household objects. Miller et.al [76] proposed a versatile simulator "GraspIt!" for robotic grasping and OpenRAVE for grasp selection. Grasp planning algorithm, while performed in cloud computing architecture can attain a greater speedup [53]. Google's goggles, a free image recognition app has been used for Robot grasping as an effective tool. Object recognition is essential for Robot Grasping where Google's object recognition engine has proved efficient. It works in two phases. In offline phase Google's goggles are used where a photo captured by a smart phone is uploaded to the Google object recognition engine to analyze and to give a list of relevant websites. However, if it cannot identify the object, a set of similar objects is returned. Lai et.al [62] proposed a modification of this system to identify objects and to determine pose, and appropriate grasp strategies in online phase. Here, the object recognition server on receipt of the photo of the object captured by the robot returns the stored data for the object. The measured 3D point set with the pressured 3D Mesh model are used to estimate pose, and selects a grasp from the set of candidate grasps. After accomplishing the grasp, the outcome is assessed and the results are stored in the cloud server for future reference [62].

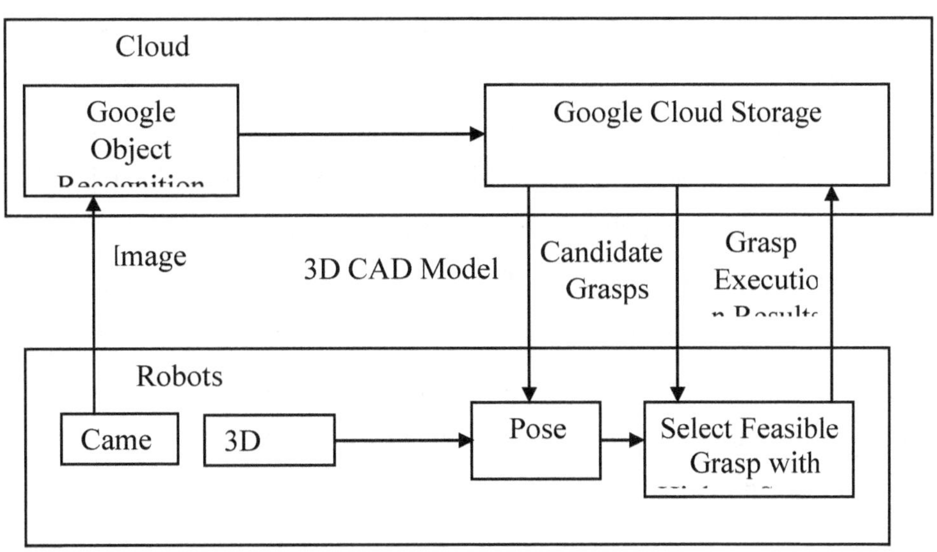

Figures 2.3 System Architecture for Cloud-based Object Recognition for Grasping [53].

A common data store for cloud means huge amounts of data which necessitates dealing with big data. Hadoop MapReduce implementation [32, 33, 36] has been found to be a widely used efficient technique to handle big data in many cases. Multi Sensor Data retrieval in Cloud Robotic systems has been designed and implemented successfully by Wang et.al [117]. Lefkowitzet.al [120] has used a twisted network framework instead of Hadoop Map Reduce contending that Map Reduce is not efficient enough for algorithms such as Parallel SLAM. Open source software plays a major role to make Cloud Robotics possible. ROS (Robot Operating System) [92] has developed an ensemble of libraries and tools which are most often used by many software developers to create robot applications.

2.4 Challenges in Cloud Robotics

Goldberget.al [30] in their survey paper, addressed in details the essential characteristics of the devices that use cloud services. Time-to-Respond (ToR) should be near real time as robotic tasks are usually time sensitive. Reliability of Response (RoR) is a key criterion of all services, as off-board computation is preferred wherein the precision and reliability of transferred data becomes crucial. The framework of data retrieval management should be compatible for different types of devices. The system in the cloud should consider the weakness of the devices that is connected to it. Hu et.al [45] has discussed the architecture challenges and applications of Cloud Robotics including the computational challenges such as what tasks to be offloaded to cloud. The decision to offload a task needs a framework that can handle issues like amount of data, delay deadline. Moreover, it should be capable enough to estimate which is advantageous, offloading or performing onboard computation [13, 19, 116]. Optimal allocation of virtual machines is also a problem of communication challenges such as the delay in communication is a major problem as robotics applications have real time requirements. Robots use wireless communication in which packet loss is very common. Security challenges exist as the robots behave according to what has been processed in the cloud. Hence, the cloud and virtual machine needs to be reliable.

Table 2.1 summarizes a few contemporary research works which highlights the issues of communications in different robot platforms involving the varied hardware devices of heterogeneous robots and hence the need for a unified and standardized data format for robot–cloud interaction.

Table2.1Research Gap

Sl.No	Author & Publication	Title	Relevance	Research Gap
1	Saha, O., & Dasgupta, P. (2018). *Robotics, 7*(3), 47. doi:10.3390/robotics7030047	A Comprehensive Survey of Recent Trends in Cloud Robotics, Architectures and Applications	Open issues and future directions	1. Issues of communications in different robot platforms 2. Need for a unified and standardized data format for robot–cloud interaction
2	Chen, W., Yaguchi, Y., Naruse, K., Watanobe, Y., Nakamura, K., & Ogawa, J. (2018), *IEEE* Access, 6, 36662-36682.	A Study of Robotic Cooperation in Cloud Robotics: Architecture and Challenges	Heterogeneity among individual robots arises from technological variation in terms of OS, software, hardware architecture, features, platform, and the communication medium	Need for a unified and standardized data format for robot–cloud interaction.
3	Mohanarajah, G., Hunziker, D., D'Andrea, R., & Waibel, M. (2014). *IEEE Transactions on Automation Science and Engineering, 12*(2), 481-493.	Rapyuta A Cloud Robotics Framework	Computing environments, which allow the robots to easily access the RoboEarth knowledge repository.	1.Confined to robots which supports Robot Operating System (ROS) 2.Use high level robot services 3.Needs high speed connectivity
4	Kehoe, B., Patil, S., Abbeel, P., & Goldberg, K. (2015). *IEEE Transactions on automation science and engineering, 12*(2), 398-409.	A Survey of Research on Cloud Robotics and Automation	Facilitates sharing of maps, images , algorithms, and hardware designs	An idea to unify knowledge database for robots to facilitate sharing.

2.5 Motivation

From the above discussions, it is observed that to make cloud robotics more efficient and simple to use, the major issue of developing some standard /unified framework for sharing and exchanging of knowledge amongst heterogeneous robots with different hardware and software has to be worked out.

In line with this, an attempt has been made in the present study to come up with a simple knowledge interchange framework for sharing information as well as a knowledge base amongst different cloud robots. The framework is validated by testing the knowledge interchange framework on different types of robots connected through cloud, mainly robots with very low configuration.

2.6 Summary

Though there are many issues in clouds such as loss of data, interruption of service, and data security [61], cloud facilitates connection of billion new devices to it [107]. Due to rapid growth of electronic devices in recent time, there are also various mobile operating systems (OS) developed to run those devices. Operating system like android OS (Google Inc.), bada (Samsung electronics), blackberry OS (Research in Motion), iphone OS/ iOS (Apple), palm OS (Garnet OS), symbian OS (Nokia), webOS (Palm/HP), windows mobile (Windows phone) are few mobile operating system commonly used for mobile devices [6]. Besides, with the evolution of Internet of Things (IOT) recently, small devices with different platforms are also able to connect and talk to each other through cloud [87]. As cloud provides a platform for devices likewise robots with less processing power will not only be able to communicate with each other but also share knowledge base redundant data through cloud.

Cloud robotics at present is still in its infancy. Researchers in this field are working and making new discoveries for sharing data and knowledge under a unified architecture. Since different robots use different platforms/OS, there are issues on compatibility, which results in redundant codes leading to unwarranted computational burden and complexities. There is a burning need for some standard /unified framework for sharing and exchanging of knowledge amongst heterogeneous robots with different hardware and software, to make cloud robotics more efficient and user friendly.

Chapter 3
Architecture of Cloud Robots

3.1 Background

Though Robots play a vital role in this technology driven era, there is a major drawback of redundancy in incorporating intelligence aspects in designing the Robot to perform. Unlike the computer systems, there are no specific standards of design for a robot. Even if the techniques to solve various robotics tasks have been implemented, yet each time a similar concept needs to be deployed, it always has to be recoded or redesigned from the scratch. Hence, various types of robots exist depending on issues like task in hand, availability of resources for the design, types of terrain for deployment of the robot etc.

The robotics community therefore has not been able to accomplish a standard guideline for the design of robots, although in all these designs the intelligent components to achieve the task appear to be similar.

To overcome this, attempts can be made to use the abstraction of the existing intelligent component from the hardware level as a vantage point from the cloud computing perspective. This layer of the intelligent component can be securely segregated and merged together as shown in the expression (3.1) below to achieve minimization of redundancy in the efforts of researchers.

$$\sum_{i=1,j=1}^{i=n,j=m} In_i \cup Hw_j \tag{3.1}$$

where In_i is the intelligence component of a robot to perform individual tasks and Hw_j represents the hardware component of the robot used to deliver the task expected out of In_i. From the expression (3.1), it can be inferred that each of the existing designs of a robot will necessarily have a redundant effort of the designer to invoke the intelligence to realize a task assigned to it. In other words, it is mandatory to have equal numbers of tasks and its associated intelligence with this model.

Conversely, if the hardware can be abstracted (which is already seen physically as well as in the mathematical model), then the component of the intelligence can be obtained from the cloud which will also enable to divert the expertise of the robot designer to formulate new intelligence components. This means that expression (3.1) can be written as

$$\sum_{i=1,j=1}^{i=n;j=m} In_j \cup Hw_i$$

where, m > n over a period of time

Here the value of n need not be necessarily equal to m, the value of m will grow exponentially over a period of time.

3.2 Cloud Robotics Architecture

Since cloud robotics applications need to be created on a platform, most designers of cloud applications prefer Robot Operating System (ROS), an open source middleware with an inter-programming language header set to enable information sharing between autonomous programs. ROS provides a graph-like structure for cloud robotics. Because robots are attached to the cloud, they can interact and exchange helpful data between themselves. The fundamental services supplied by Cloud Computing include massive parallel computing and information sharing in real time.

Middleware Robot is an abstraction layer between the operating system and the software application that manages hardware heterogeneity, enhances software application's performance, simplifies software design and reduces production expenses. ROS can be termed as one such middleware. Elkady and Sobh [21], in their discussion on Robotics Middleware, described the objectives of ROS as a middleware which provides services of the operating system such as low-level device control, hardware abstraction, message-passing between processes, and many others. So, ROS is not an operating system but a "metaoperating system" [92] for robot software which consists of a number of small tools to allow sharing of data between independent programs. In other words, ROS is an open source robot operating system that provides Hardware abstraction, Low-level device control, Message Passing and Package Management. Willow Garage [91] preserves ROS as an open source project which offers a graph-like pattern for networked robotics. It was developed by Stanford in 2007 under the name Switchyard [5] originally. It provides package tools and operating system like tools [108]. ROS allows independent, individual programs, referred to in ROS nomenclature as nodes, to share data between themselves [14]. ROS is based on nodes, messages, topics, and services, wherein the nodes are the software modules or processes in the control code which communicate with each other through message passing and/or passing multiple messages. A special type of message, called service, consists of a pair of messages, one for request and the other for reply. Nodes can publish and subscribe to a single (or multiple) topics.

ROS can be used to create robots for the daily purposes while Cloud Robotics can help in augmenting the information contained in these robots. So, basically, ROS is used to develop robotic applications and Cloud Robotics to maintain them. It is interesting to note that the Personal Robot 2 (PR2) is a portable manipulation platform built by Willow Garage [94] wherein the entire software (PR2) structure is written with the help of ROS enabling all PR2 capabilities being available to use via ROS interfaces. So, Cloud robotics using ROS is not too far from sight. In days to come, ROS can be used to develop robotic applications that will work with the cloud. Moreover, the choice of ROS over other Robotic middleware can be preferred because it is much more easy to use and is flexible. ROS being an open-source platform for robot software development, it is all the more easy to maintain.

Since the primary goal of ROS is to support code reuse in robotics research and development [92], it suits better for cloud robotics so that code created for one robot can easily be reused in others too.

Figure 3.1 depicts the scenario wherein each robot existed as a standalone machine with minimal interaction. Figure 3.2 represents the coexistence of multi-robots and their knowledge base improvement over a time. Hence robots would be cheaper, smarter and more efficient when cloud computing techniques are adopted by incorporating a minimal interface which does not compromise on the existing individual techniques of fabrication.

The interface shown in Figure 3.2 is similar to the concept suggested in RoboEarth [80], where robots share intelligence with Robot Operating System (ROS). Since all the robots do not support any fixed standard ROS, the interface depicted in this chapter is a novel effort to test robots running in different operating system. Apart from ROS, some robots have processors such as Boebot- BASIC Stamp and Lego NXT-Atmel AT91SAM7S256 microcontroller which does not support interfaces for fast data transfer.

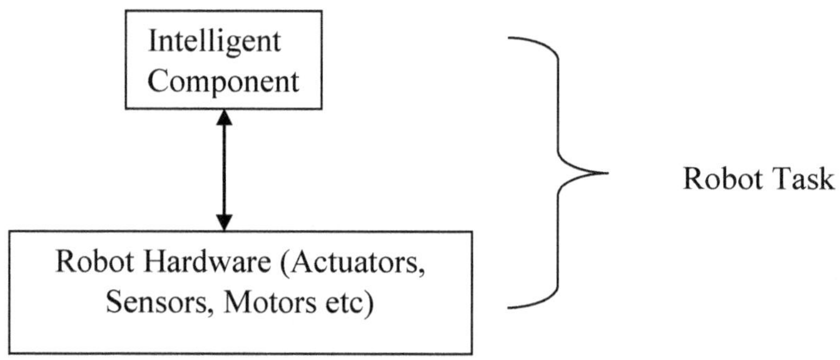

Figure 3.1: Components of a Robot for each assigned task.

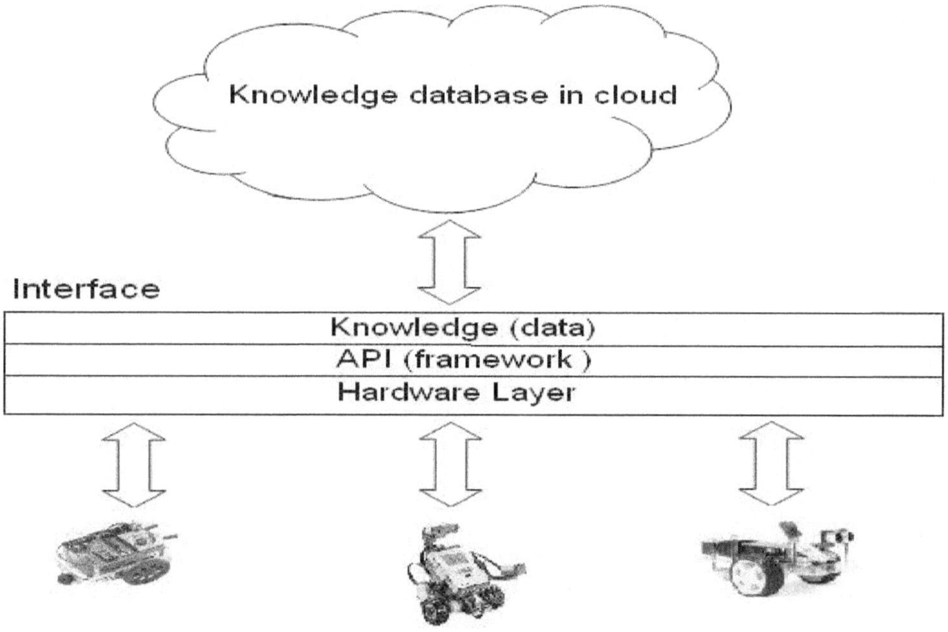

Figure3.2 Set of Intelligent Components extracted from the Cloud by the Individual Robot through an Interface.

A comparative study of some of the communication mediums and their drawbacks are summarized in Tables 3.1-2-3 below.

Table 3.1 shows the comparison in terms of range, speed of connection and model of communication when connection devices like Bluetooth, WiFi and GSM are used. It implies that the proposed interface unit should be in proximity with the robot. Since speed is device dependent, data transfer is limited to avoid high latency in a real time environment.

Table 3.1 Comparison of Performances of Device Based Communication.

Device used	Range	Speed	Model
Bluetooth	Low (30 feet approx.)	low speed	Proxy-based
Wi-Fi	Medium (300 feet approx.)	high speed	Peer based
GSM	World wide	medium speed	Peer based/Proxy

Table 3.2 Comparison of various Modes of Communications.

Communication mode	Model	Programming level
Through middleware	Proxy-based, peer based	Low level-Speed ,distance calculation High level – Use of API's
Through gateway	Peer based	Low level-Speed, distance calculation High level – Use of API's

Table 3.2 depicts the mode of communications between robots and cloud. It also shows the kind of communication model that can be achieved depending on the communication mode.

Table 3.3 below shows the comparison based on the type of services the cloud robot can provide. As storage as a robotics service, robots are able to store knowledge databases in the cloud instead of storing it in its own local memory. This model helps robots to share intelligence gathered through a shared memory in the cloud.

Table 3.3 Comparisons of various Services Model Based Communications.

Service Model	Interchange format processor	Types of services	Programming level	Speed
Storage as a service	Needed	Store Knowledge database. e.g. The proposed KIF	Low level- Speed distance calculation	Fast(50-100 ms)
Software as a service	Not Needed	Image processing, voice processing etc.	High level – Use of API's	Slow (5-30 secs)

Table 3.4 summarizes some of the existing technologies available and services provided by cloud. The columns with tick marks are the technologies implemented in this thesis.

Table 3.4 Existing Technologies and Services Provided by Cloud.

Type of Communication /Services	Available	Used
Wireless	1. Bluetooth	√
	2. GSM	√
	3. Zigbee	X
	4. LORA WAN	X
	5. WiFi	√
Communication with Cloud	1. Middleware	√
	2. Gateway	√
Services	Iaas	√
	Paas	X
	Saas	√

3.3 Summary of the Chapter

In this Chapter, a generic architecture is discussed wherein robots can be linked through the cloud with various communication technologies. Though the concept of sharing knowledge is already implemented in RoboEarth [80], the difficulties in dealing with different processors which do not support ROS or connection devices with low data transfer rate are also addressed in this chapter.

Chapter 4

Knowledge Interchange Format (KIF) for the Heterogeneous Robots to Communicate on the Generic Architecture

4.1 Background

The most important factor for a mobile robot is to increase the knowledge to share what has been learnt so that the robots can solve day-to-day problems by learning as and when required. *Knowledge sharing facilitates robots to accomplish tasks that individual robots could not have accomplished.*

Since the robots used for knowledge sharing are not homogeneous, the architecture and the support for languages vary largely. A language/instruction set recognized by one robot may not be recognized by another robot. In such a scenario, it is essential that the robots share a common type of representation. A Knowledge Interchange Format (KIF) [26] is usually meant for the interchange of knowledge among different computer programs. While reading a knowledge base in KIF, a program converts the data into its specific internal form of pointer structures, arrays, etc. to perform the computations internally, which are then mapped into the common format *viz;* KIF to communicate with another program. Thus, it can also be used for exchange of knowledge between the robots of different architectures. Hence, *a Knowledge Interchange Format (KIF)* plays a vital role in enabling the robots of different hardware to interpret a common format easily without much complexity, even in case of robots with lesser hardware configurations. Though there are several ways of representing knowledge interchange format for robots as mentioned in [97, 98], a parametric representation which deals with the low level representation is considered for masking the heterogeneity to an extent.

The knowledge in this Test bed is a 'map representation' in the form of a continuous variable string represented in the form of a path taken by a robot. It is assumed that the robot moves in open control loop an ideal condition where there are no dynamic obstacles and no odometry error on the wheel. Considering a robot takes only left, right, back or front, a representation of the path is discussed below.

The general format of the variable string considered is:
[Distance/Angle] [Direction]…..[Stop]

For example, the string **50F90L60B45R30FS** will cause the robot to move a distance of 50 cm forward, then turn Left and traverse 90 cm, then 60 cm Backward (reverse which is represented as "B" instead of "R" for reverse to avoid ambiguity with Right), then take Right turn and move 45cm then again 30 cm forward and S is the delimiter for stopping the robot in an open control loop.

Considering the speed and time of any robot to be constant, the distance covered by a robot can be calculated using the diameter of the wheel of the robot for different robots.

When the path gets stored in cloud, the destination and source gets added at the front of the string and all the intermediate nodes are added so that the string will look like
ab|50Lc60B40Rh30FS|
where,

ab= source destination pair

|= delimiter

A score/weight is added after the last delimiter '|'to assign or choose the likeability of paths. The integer value represents the distance.

4.2 Representation of paths

To explain the environment with different stations and paths, an example with destination 'b' and source 'a' and two paths is shown in Figure 4.1, wherein the String 55Rc105F15Rh55FS represents one of the path from 'a' to 'b' marked by the thin line while the String 70Bd100Rg55FS represents the other path from 'a' to 'b' marked by the bold thick line.

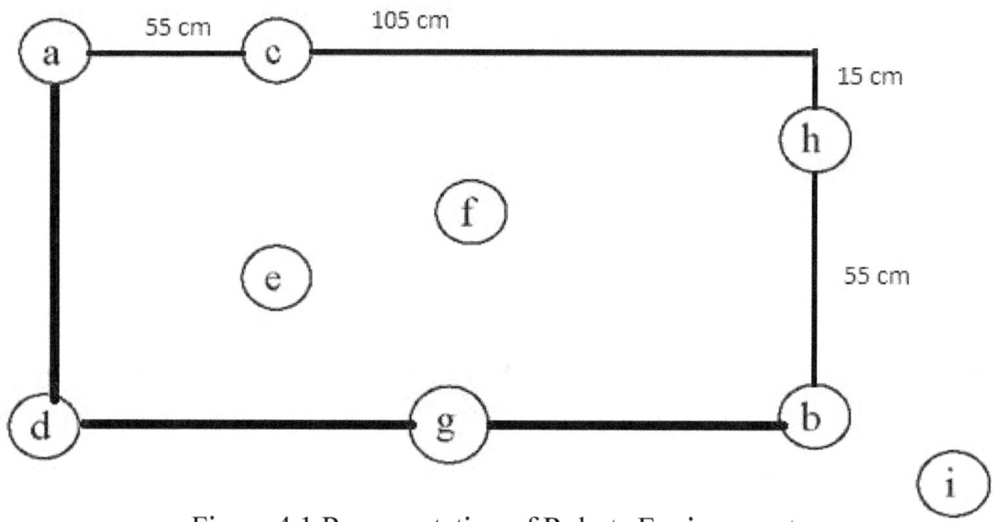

Figure 4.1 Representation of Robots Environment

In the bold thick line of Figure 4.1, the source is 'a' and the destination is 'b', and 'c' and 'h' are two intermediate nodes. There might be situations where robots need the path from 'c' to 'h', so it becomes necessary to list the intermediate nodes in the representation. The details of intermediate nodes in the representation have been provided by writing it in small letters to uniquely identify that it is an intermediate node. The representation of bold line will now be as ab|55Rc105F15Rh55FS| which implies that 'a' is the source, 'b' is the destination, after moving 55 cm right it reaches c and it moves 105 cm forward and then takes a right turn and moves 15cm to reach h and then finally reaches 'b' after moving forward for 55 cm and then stops.

For the simplicity of searching the paths from intermediate nodes after the first delimiter, the list of intermediate nodes are added after it and is represented as:
ab| ch|55Rc105F15Rh55FS|9.
In the above given string

- 'a' is the source.
- 'b' is the destination.
- 'c' and 'h' are the intermediate nodes.
- Robot starts from 'a' and moves 55 cms right to reach 'c'.
- Robot then moves 105 cms forward and then 15 cms right to reach h.
- From 'h' it moves 55 cms forward and then stops at 'b'.
- Number after the last delimiter is the score generated after processing.

4.3 Processing of Paths and testing it in Hadoop MapReduce

Most often, the data gathered during traversing and finding paths by the robot is very large. As there will be a collection of large no of paths, these data will eventually form big data and are usually stored in the Cloud. Since the traditional computing techniques cannot be used to process these data sets, the parallel processing technique Hadoop Map Reduce is commonly used to process the paths in parallel [33].

Map Reduce is a highly parallelized programming model that can be used for processing large data sets. The task of partitioning the input data, scheduling the programs execution in different clusters, making it fault tolerant, and managing inter machine communication is taken care by the run time system [33].

The open source framework Hadoop [33] written in Java provides distributed storage and computation over a cluster of computers with simple programming models. It has the capability of scaling up from a single server to thousands of machines with local computation and storage each. Hadoop has been set up in standalone mode on Ubuntu 14.04 system. The setup runs on a single Java Virtual Machine (jvm). It becomes easy to test and debug the map reduce programs. Less amount of sample sets are used so that the default properties are set for standalone mode to run the map reduce programs. 10 sample paths as shown below have been generated for the environment.

ab|10L5Rc20R50Fg50fS|0

ab|10L5R20Re70FS|0

ag|50L12Rf10Fh20BS|0

ab|10L5Rc20R50F25B20Rh50fS|0

vk|30L20Ru10Bw10RS|0

ab|30R10Lr25RS|0

ab|10L5Rc20Rd50Fe25Bf20Rg50fS|0

gk|5Rh10Li20BS|0

vk|20Rl10LS|0

ab|10L20Rd50FS|0

In the above strings, the zero in the last field indicates that the paths that have never been shared or processed. Once the request for any source destination pair is made, a Map Reduce is used to find all the strings that match the required source destination pair. There might be many intermediate nodes between the source and destination Hence the entire string has been checked to find the paths that might be intermediate nodes. To find all the paths matching some pattern there is no need to combine intermediate key-value pairs and hence Reduce is not needed. Map takes path and outputs if it matches the pattern. This is not a good idea if there is a single large document, but works well if there are many documents. In a realistic scenario there might be many documents as there may be a large number of robots. Therefore the use of Map Reduce is justified.
The processing of the path requires the following stages:

a) The purpose of Map Driver class are as follows:

i) Provide the mapper class name
ii) Provide the reducer class name
iii) Provide file input format in key and value pairs
iv) Provide file output format in key value pairs
v) Provide output key class
vi) Provide value key class

It is generally used for giving configuration information.

b) Path Mapper Class: The purpose of mapper class is to split the word on basis of delimiter (the delimiter is |) and search 'ab' pair. Then sum the total cost.
Shuffling and sorting is done automatically by map reduce framework. It is done on the basis of total cost (in ascending order) of individual input.

c) Path Reducer Class: It takes the output from Path Mapper, after shuffling and sorting, merges result and gives the output.

4.4 MapDriver Class

The task of map driver class is to control the entire job. It is the top-level class and the main entry point. The main function in this class takes commands by an argument which is, the input, output file and the source destination pair.

The job object gets instantiated. File input format and file output format describes the input and output specification for the job and creates path objects based on arguments variable. The output path gets created by Map Reduce job and output files are deposited there. The behavior for file input format is to read key value text separated by delimiter. WaitForCompletion method is called. This method launches the job and returns success or not. Upon success, the mapper and reducer class are called.Mapper is the base class which is used to implement the Map tasks. The input to mapper class is a key-value pair and the output is an intermediate key-value pair. The reducer takes the intermediate key-value pair and merges the result after sorting and shuffling. The flowchart for Mapdriver class is shown in Figure 4.2. The framework handles all the details of the numbers of mappers required and how to read distributed input file.

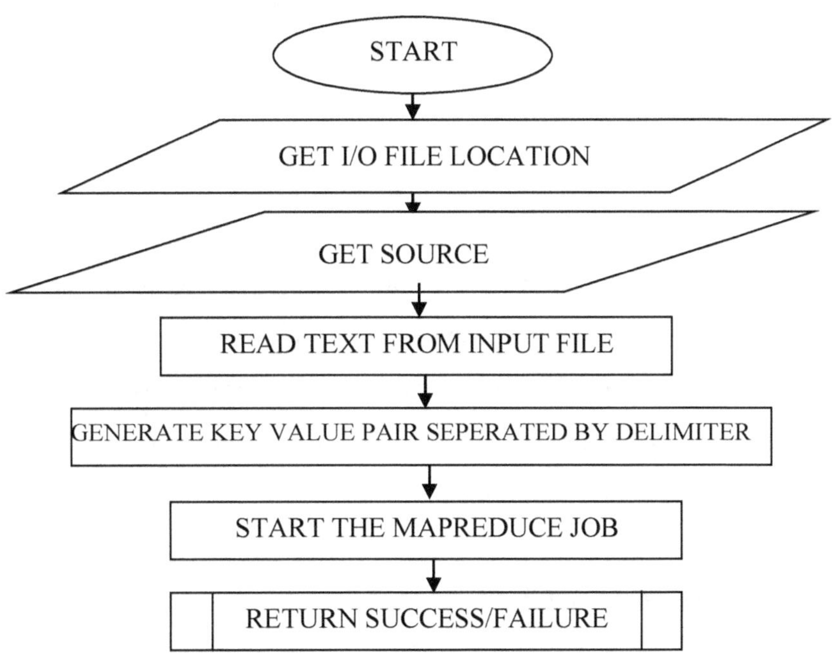

Figure 4.2 Flowchart of MapDriver,

4.5 PathMapper Class

PathMapper extends the Mapper class to implement the map function. In a distributed computing model, data gets sent from node to node via Remote Procedure Call and data must be serialized and deserialized as it goes. Hadoop built-in data serialization format is called writable. Writable class exists as a wrapper for almost all Java primitive types. Some java primitives with their writable implementation are shown in Table.4.1.

The declaration for the costumed Mapper class extends the class Mapper. The Mapper class uses parameterized types to define the types of key values for both input and output. The input key and input values are text, output keys are text and output values are integers. To implement map function, map method is overridden.

Table 4.1 Writable Implementation of Java Primitive Data Types.

Java Primitive	**Writable Implementation**
Boolean	"BooleanWritable"
byte	"ByteWritable"
Int	"IntWritable"
float	"FloatWritable"
long	"LongWritable"
Double	"DoubleWritable"

The map function searches if source and destination exists in the representation. If source and destination exists then the distance from source to destination is calculated by parsing the string and a list of key value pairs where key is the string from source to destination and value is the distance to reach from source to destination. The flowchart for PathMapper is shown in Figure 4.3.

4.6 PathReducer Class

The PathReducer class extends the class reducer. Just like the Mapper the reducer class uses parameterized types to define the keys and values. The input and output key are text

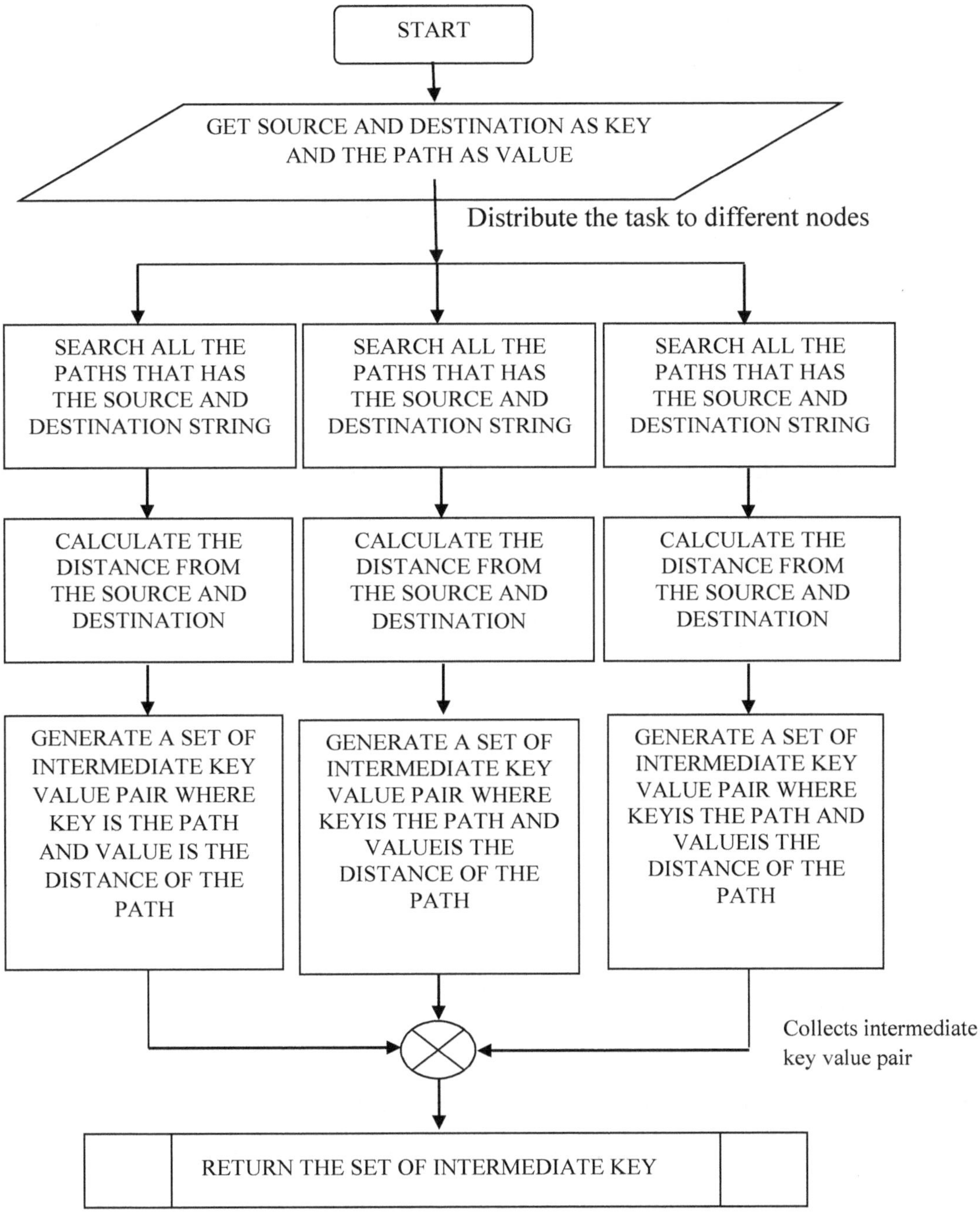

Figure 4.3 Flowcharts for PathMapper

whereas the input and output values are integers. To implement the reduce function reduce method is overridden. The reduce function distributes the key value pairs to various nodes, where based on value the paths are sorted at each step. The sorting technique used here is merge sort. At each node, merge sort is done and later the results from each node are compared and combined. The sorted data from each node are checked with each other to finally output the sorted data. These data are stored in the output file at the location provided by MapDriver class. The flowchart for path reducer is shown in Figure. 4.4.

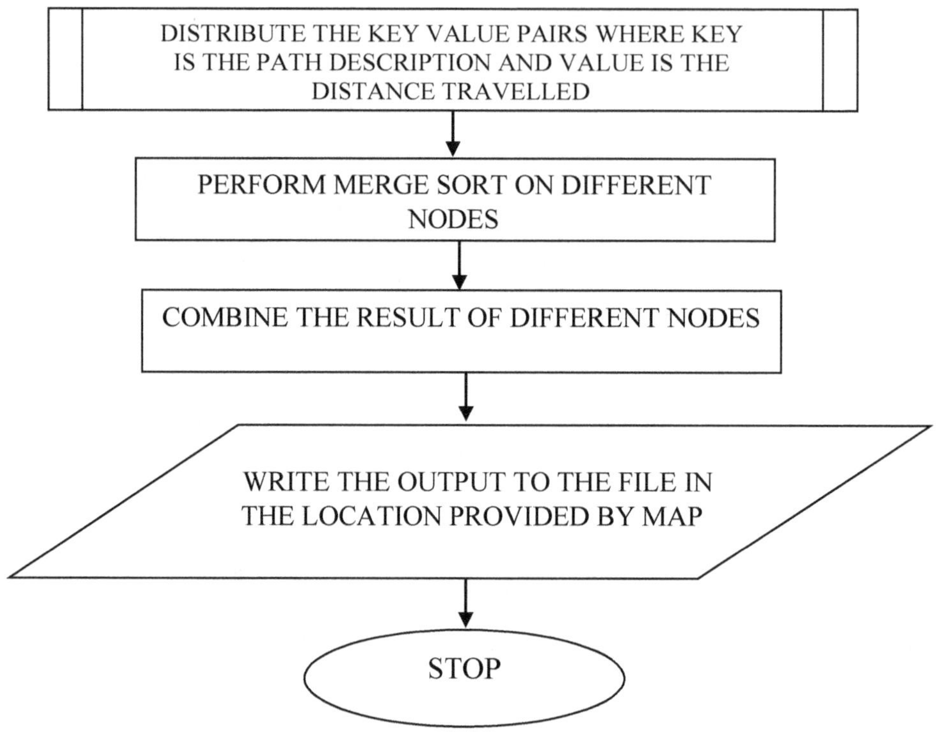

Figure 4.4 Flowchart of PathReducer.

4.7 Execution on Hadoop Cluster

The above mentioned processes viz., MapDriver Class, PathMapper Class and Path Reducer Class, which are also known as Hadoop Cluster, are executed in parallel after taking the source from the driver class as shown below in Fig 4.5.

4.8 Weights Assignments

The distance from source to destination is calculated by adding each integer value that exists in path representation. The distance is added at the end of the string based on the distance the strings are sorted. Once the file contains sorted strings, weights are assigned to each strings, where w=r-p; r is the reward assigned to each string depending upon the shortest distance in descending order and penalty p is assigned in reverse order. If there are n number of paths, then the value of p =1 and r=n for path with the shortest distance. Next time if the robot needs the path to the same source destination pair then it can choose the path with highest weights and in case if there is some problem with the weight i.e. the path is broken or any obstacle is found then the robot can request the path that has the next high weights. Table.4.2 shows the generation of weights for 5 different paths from ‘a’ to ‘b’.

Table 4.2 Generating Score for Paths.

Path	Penalty(p)	Reward (r)	Weight(r - p)
ab|30R10Lr25RS|65	1	5	4
ab|10L20Rd50FS|80	2	4	2
ab|10L5R20Re70FS|105	3	3	0
ab|10L5Rc20R50Fg50FS|135	4	2	-2
ab|10L5Rc20Rd50Fe25Bf20Rg50FS|180	5	1	-4

The input sample set is stored in a text file path.txt and copied to Hadoop file system.

ab|10L5Rc20R50Fg50FS|0

ab|10L5R20Re70FS|0

ag|50L12Rf10Fh20BS|0

ac|10L5RS|0

vk|30L20Ru10Bw10RS|0

ab|30R10Lr25RS|0

gk|5Rh10Li20BS|0

vk|20Rl10LS|0

ab|10L20Rd50FS|0

ab|10L5Rc20Rd50Fe25Bf20Rg50FS|0

Reduce program is run on Hadoop clusters where the location of input file and output file is provided by arguments. The program is run to find the paths from source a to destination b. The intermediate key value pairs after finding distance from a to b. The reducer takes the key value pair generated by map function and sorts the value using merge sort which is combined to generate the required output. Figure 4.5 shows the input output and the intermediate key value pairs generated at each step of MapReduce. The Mapper searches for all the paths from a to b and generates

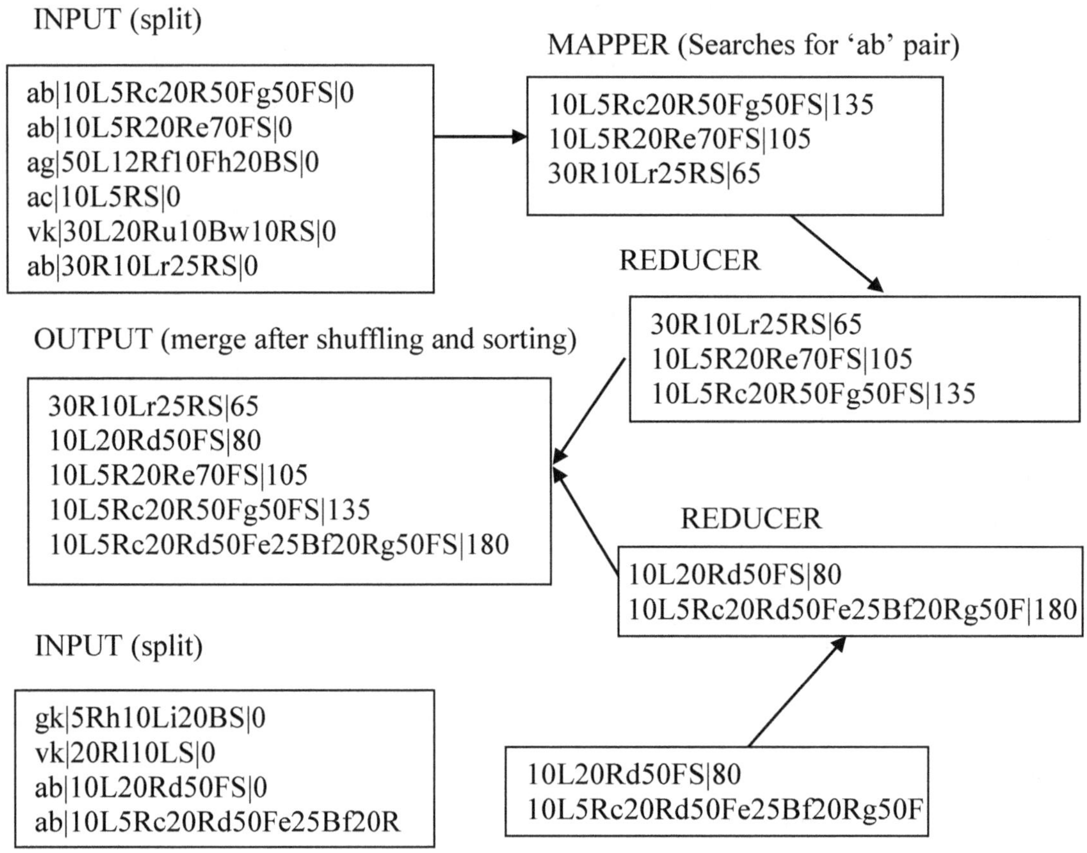

Figure 4.5 Results of MapReduce programs

4.9 Summary of the Chapter

The main objective of this chapter is to introduce a Knowledge Interchange Format (KIF) or *variable length string* for the heterogeneous robots to communicate on the generic architecture. Emphasis has been given to generate a representation of path for robots (keeping in mind the size of data) that can be processed in parallel and saved in the cloud, enabling sharing of knowledge between robots. A variable length string data interchange format is considered for representing a path. Representation is made simple for compatibility across all microprocessors. The variable length string is tested in Hadoop Map Reduce to simulate cloud processing.

Chapter 5

Cloud-Enabled Robotic Framework for Fixed Length String

5.1 Background

In order to test the proposed architecture of Cloud-Enabled Robotic Framework, as discussed in chapter 3, a test bed for fixed length string communication has been proposed and developed wherein a middleware has been used as an interface unit. Fixed string here refers to alpha-numeric string converted from standard bar-code viz; EAN-13 (a 13 digits code used in barcodes). The architecture is illustrated with a case study of cloud enabled robotic framework for a Library Assistant as Test bed – I for automatic sorting of books by robots exploiting the rich database of books from the cloud.

Nicolas Oros and Jeffrey L. Krichmar [82], have mentioned android-based robots. Available open source platforms developed for Android phones can be used to control different robotic platforms. Various examples have shown that Android phones could be used as an onboard computer for the existing robots. 'Robots Everywhere' is a company which uses open source software to control the robots for Android based robots [15]. Google Inc. has also developed android robot libraries [2]. Some libraries called Cellbots for Android and Python have been already listed out [113]. So, the gap between android and robotic applications could be bridged so as to create an application that could make the two technologies work hand in hand to sort library books. Android applications can be created to control robots and make them perform many other tasks in the future.

In view of above, an attempt has been made to develop a cloud architecture comprising middleware (on an android application) which acts as an interface for communication between the cloud infrastructure and the robot. Standard Application Programming Interface (API) has been used to harness the database and computing power of cloud.

5.2 Test Bed I: Through Fixed Length String

Test Bed 1 is a cloud-enabled robot to sort books by scanning barcodes. The whole experiment is divided into two basic components - the middleware (android component) and the robot interface. The two components work hand-in-hand with each other to enable sorting and placing of books in the respective shelves.

The middleware component scans the barcode of a book and sends it to the cloud (using Google Books API) for information retrieval. The type information that it receives from the cloud is then used to decide the movement of the robot. After segregating the book into a certain type, it communicates with the robot over communication medium (Bluetooth serial data transmission) to send the shelf number.

The robot receiver (which is a Bluetooth module), receives serial data, i.e. shelf number, from the middleware (android device). It then grabs the book, lifts it up, and then moves the book to its corresponding shelf. The path to a particular shelf is assumed to be pre-defined. After keeping the book on its shelf, it returns to its default position.

5.3 Architecture

The architecture of this experiment is divided into two components – the middleware (android) interface and the robotics control system (Boebot).

The main task of the middleware (android interface) is to recognize books in the library by scanning their barcodes with the help of a barcode scanning library. In this study, ZXing scanner library [126] in android programming is used that makes use of the barcode scanner app to scan barcodes in the EAN-13 format.

The next subtask is to sort the books according to available book details. To achieve this, the system is connected to the Google Books API with a private key. After scanning the barcode, the middleware interface reads and then sends the ISBN to the cloud i.e. Google API for information retrieval. On receipt of the ISBN, the cloud sends back all the available information related to that particular book, *viz;* author's name and title of the book, book-edition, publisher's name, year of publications etc. According to these details, the android application categorizes books into different categories.

After segregating the book into a certain category, it communicates with the robot over transmitter (Bluetooth serial data transmission) to send the shelf number. To accomplish this task, a connection is established between the middleware (android) applications to the robot (Boebot).

The other subtask is to make the Robot (Boebot) move according to the movement instruction sent by the middleware (android application). As per the information sent via the transmitter (Bluetooth), the robot (Boebot) moves forward to grab the book (object) and move to its correct shelf with the help of its wheels and then it returns to its default position. The process repeats until all the books are sorted and arranged in different shelves.

Detection of objects was done with the help of an IR LED that is placed at the center-front of the Robot (Boebot). Right behind it is an IR sensor that detected the radiation reflected from the object detected. The IR (Infrared) LED and sensor is used to emit and detect the radiation in the robot (Boebot) respectively.

5.4 Setting up of Test Bed I

5.4.1 Testing the Boebot

Though the main parts of the Boebot are already connected to the chassis but to ensure that the servomotors are properly aligned and connected to the chassis at the time of experiment, centering of the servo motor has been ensured by BASIC stamp program. While the servomotor is running, the internal potentiometer is adjusted so as to stop motors turning to ensure that PULSOUT 12, 750 or PULSOUT 13, 750 would be the center position. Here, 12 and 13 refer to Right and Left motors respectively and 750 refers to the angular velocity, so that a value greater than 750 would turn the motor one way, while a value less than 750 would turn it another way. Hence, the Boebot is made ready to move.

Initially Boebot is communicated using the serial cable. Wireless communication is then established between Android devices with an inbuilt Bluetooth and Boebot with the wireless communication card on the Boebot, the Easy Bluetooth module (eb500) [44].

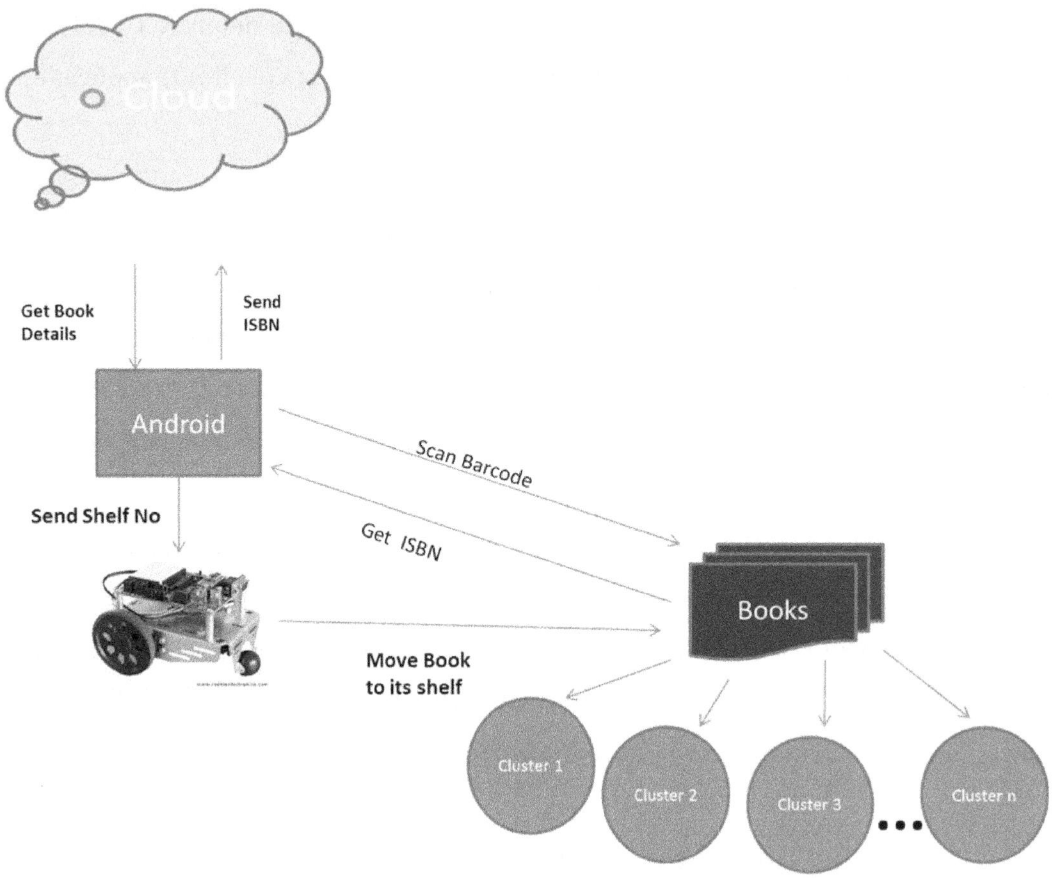

Figure 5.1 Architecture of Cloud Enabled Robot for Sorting Books.

5.4.2 Testing the Android App

The Barcode Scanner application ZXinglibrary [126] has been tested separately before integration and then integrated to the android application. Next, Bluetooth communication with the Boebot has been incorporated.

The android application had two different modules altogether. The modules have been integrated to function as one single unit. 'Preview' functionality for the book, after barcode scanning has been added. A HTML page has also been implemented to display the preview of the scanned book. Figure 5.2 below depicts the flowchart of interactions of various modules in the architecture.

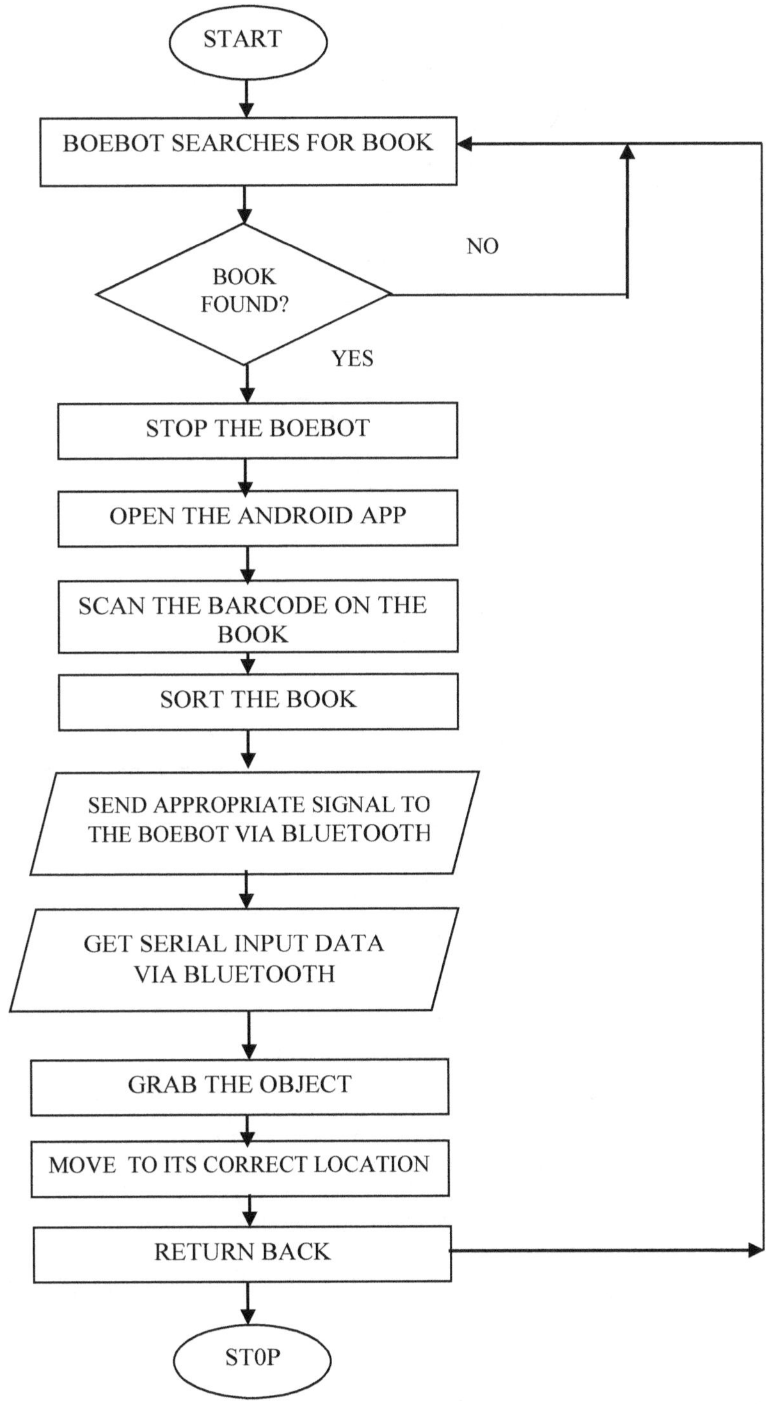

Figure 5.2 Flowchart of the Robot's Task/Activities

The flow charts of the activities of Boebot are divided into two parts as shown in Figures 5.3 and 5.4 below.

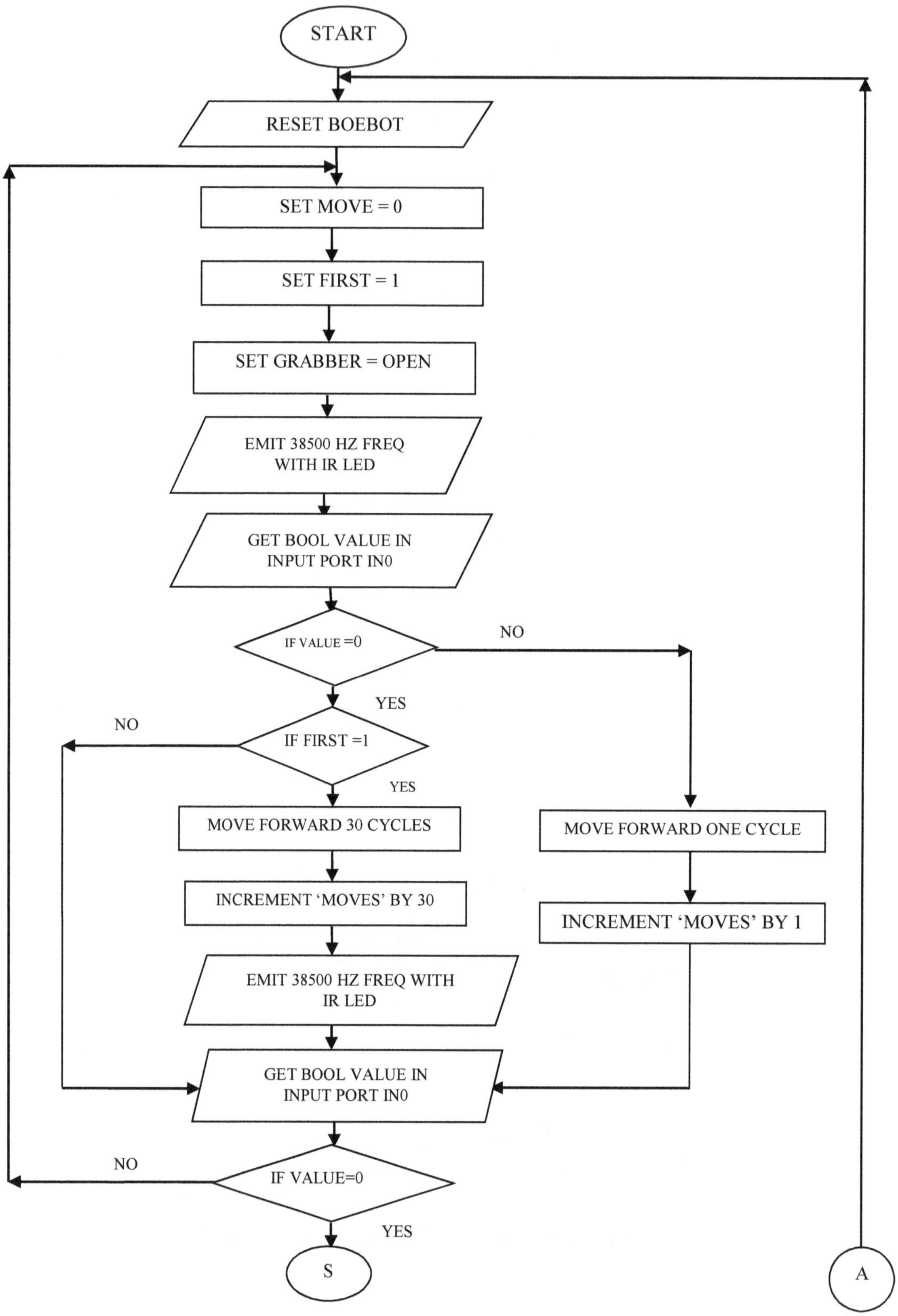

Figure 5.3 Flowchart for Boebot (Part I)

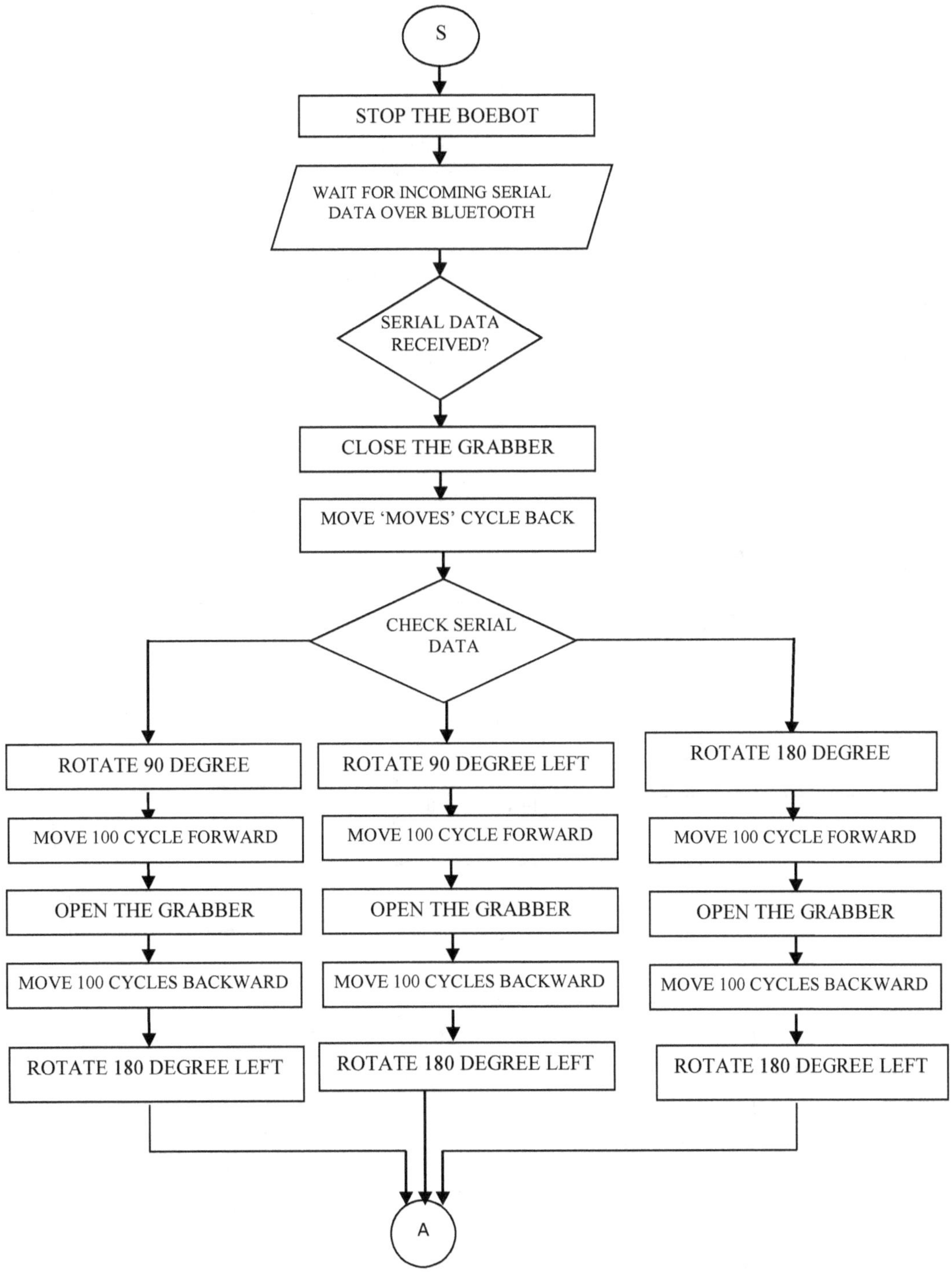

Figure 5.4 Flowchart for Boebot (Part II)

It consists of identifying a book and getting a command from the middleware through its Bluetooth module.

Figure 5.5 below presents the flowchart for the communication between the middleware (an android app developed for the purpose) and the cloud through GSM module.

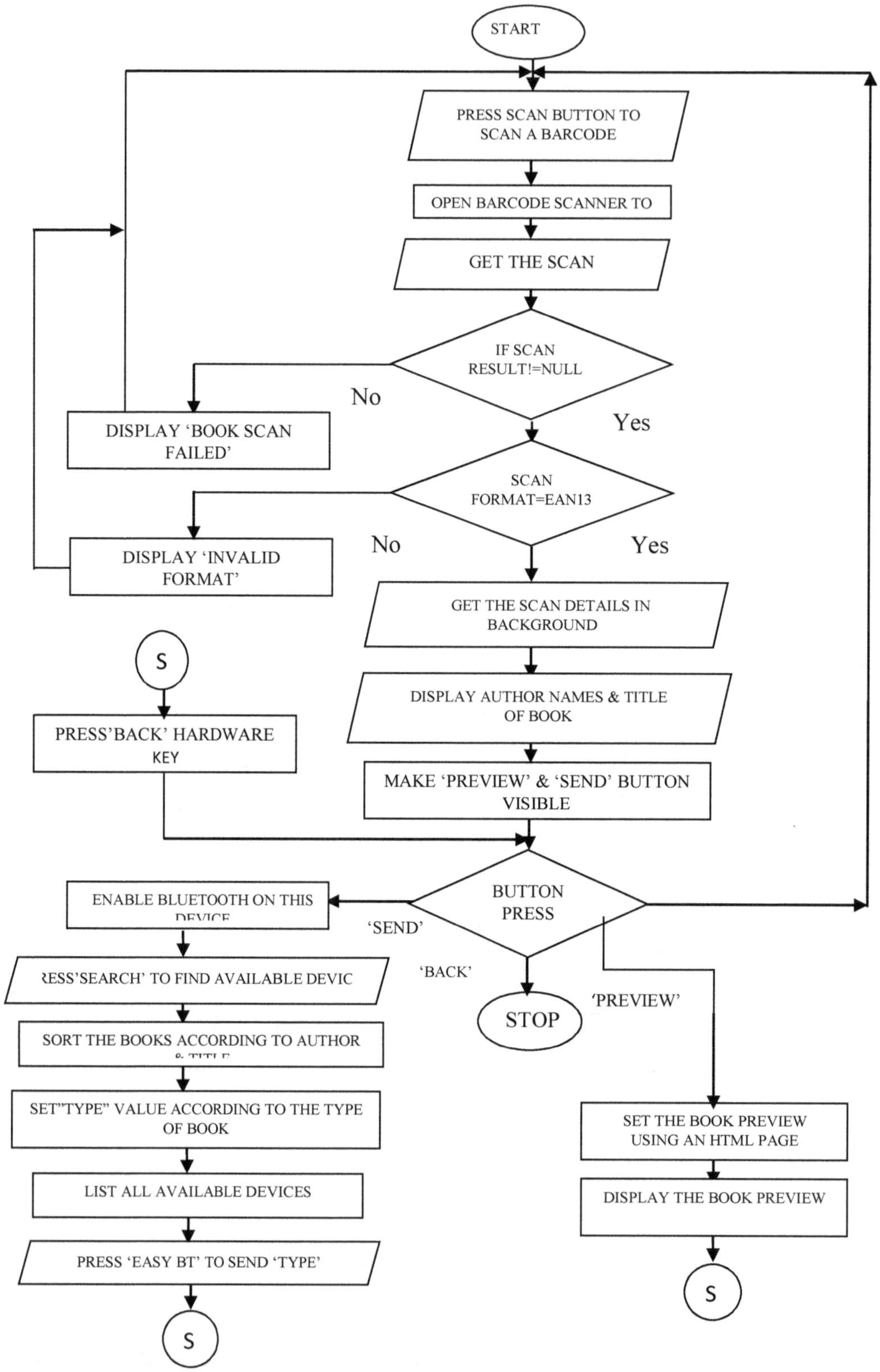

Figure 5.5 Flowchart for communication between middleware and the cloud through GSM module

5.5 Implementation

The experiment has been successfully implemented using Barcodes of books. Barcode is a very good and efficient way to find information about the books using the Google Books API. Connecting robots to the cloud makes it possible to exploit the enormous resources of the cloud in terms of storage and computing powers. Thereby making robots no longer be limited by their own individual memories and programs [93].

The next phase dealt with the reception of shelf number by the Boebot using Bluetooth transmission and moving to the correct shelf. Alongside, in android programming, other aspects of the experiment include Bluetooth device scanning, pairing, and sending data.

The last phase of the programming involves the linking of all the modules into one. The Bluetooth module with the barcode scanner module of the android program has been linked in this phase [15]. The whole experiment is linked as the android application scanned the barcode, sends the barcode detail to the Google Books API, gets back the book details, sorts the books according to the book detail, and sends the shelf number to the Boebot's easy Bluetooth module via Bluetooth transmission. The Boebot first scanned the area for any book-like object. If it found one, it stopped for the instruction of the android application. After getting the shelf number, it grabbed the book and moved to the appropriate shelf and returned back to its home position.

Accordingly, the test has been implemented in two different programming paradigms. One was the low-level robot programming, and another was the high-level android device programming. The android programming language using "Eclipse editor" is used for the android application and the PBasic programming language viz; "Basic Stamp2" is used for programming the microprocessor in the robot. The algorithms for the two modules are given in the next section. The pseudo codes for the modules are given in *Appendix V (Pseudo Code for Boebot) and Appendix VI (Pseudo Code for Android Barcode Scanner).*

5.5.1 Algorithm for Robot (Boebot)

Step 1: Start

Step 2: Reset Boebot

Step 3: Set move to 0

Step 4: Set first to 1

Step 5: Set grabber to open

Step 6: Emit 38500 Hz freq with infrared light emitting diode

Step 7: Get the Boolean value in the input port

Step 8: if value is not 0, go to step 13

Step 9: if first is not 1 one, go to step 13

Step 10: Move forward 30 cycles

Step 11: Increment 'moves, by 30

Step 12: Emit 38500 Hz freq with infrared light emitting diode

Step 13: Get Boolean value in input port

Step 14: If value is not 0 goto step 3

Step 15: Stop the Boebot

Step 16: Wait for incoming serial data over Bluetooth

Step 17: Close the grabber

Step 18: Move 'moves' cycle back

Step 19: Case 1: Rotate 90 degree right // for shelf no. 1

Move 100 cycle forward

Open the grabber

Move 100 cycles backward

Rotate the Boebot 90 degree left

Goto step no. 2

Step 20: Case 2: Rotate 90 degree left // for shelf no. 2

Move 100 cycle forward

Open the grabber

Move 100 cycles backward

Rotate the Boebot 90 degree right

Goto step no. 2

Step 21: Case 2: Rotate 180 degree // for shelf no. 3

Move 100 cycle forward

Open the grabber

Move 100 cycles backward

Rotate the Boebot 180 degree

Goto step no. 2

5.5.2 Algorithm for interface device (for Android App)

Step 1: Start

Step 2: Press button to scan barcode

Step 3: Open barcode scanner to scan

Step 4: Get the scan result

Step 5: If the scan result is equal to null, display 'book scan failed', goto step 2

Step 6: If the scan format is not EAN 13 display ' invalid format', goto step 3

Step 7: Get the details of the book

Step 8: Display author name and title of the book

Step 9: Sort the book according to author name and title of the book

Step 10: Send the appropriate shelf number to the Boebot through Bluetooth

Step 11: If all the books are not scanned, goto to step2

Step 12: Stop

5.6 Snap Shots

To highlight the operations and performance of the experiment conducted, some of the snapshots of the various functions are shown below.

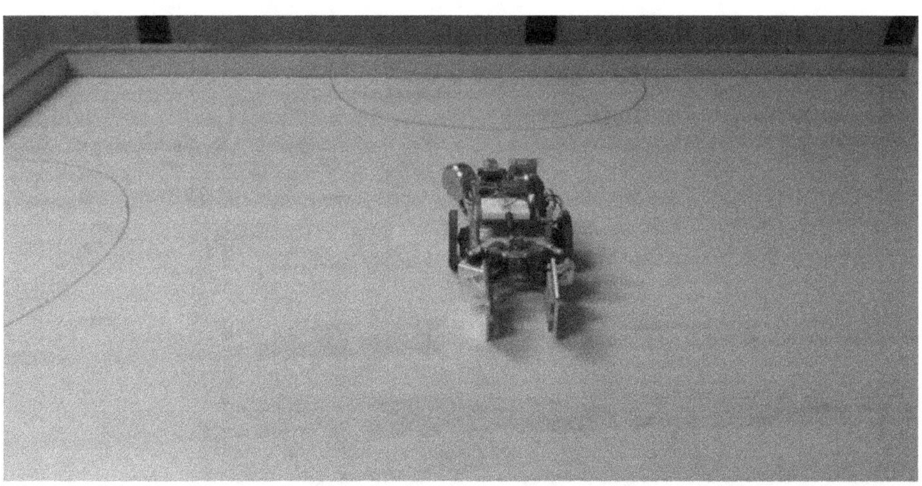

Figure 5.6 The Boebot is Ready to Search for the Books and Scan their Barcodes.

Figure 5.7 Boebot Stops when it Detects an Object.

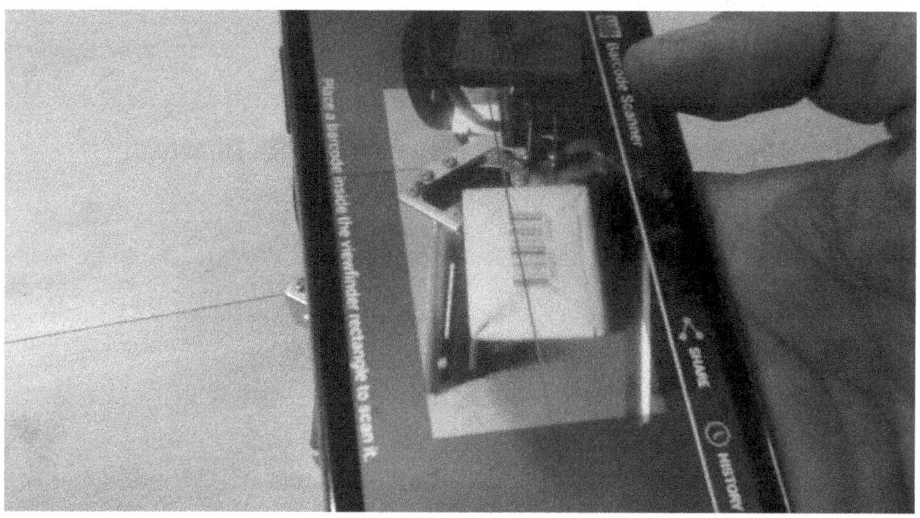

Figure 5.8 Android Application Scanning the Barcode in a Book.

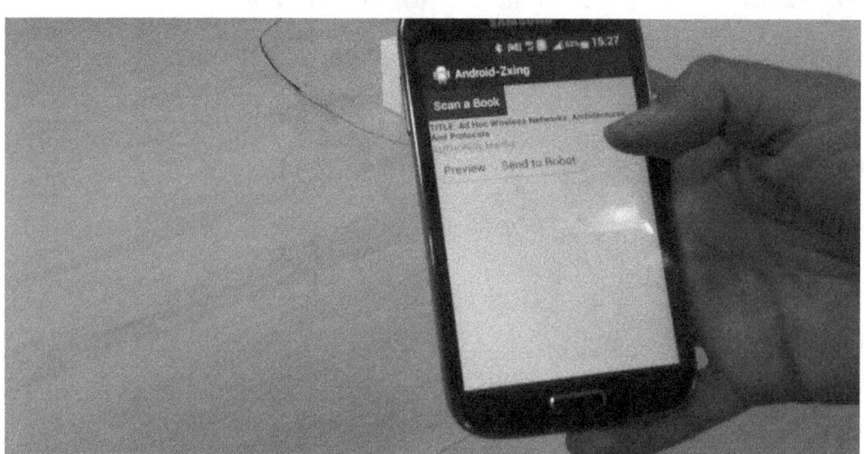

Figure 5.9 Android Application getting the Details of the Book from the Cloud.

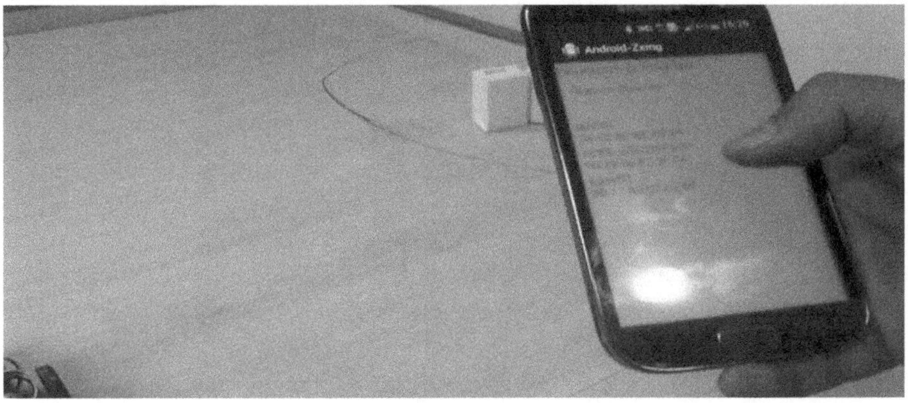

Figure 5.10 Android Application Searching for Active Bluetooth Devices.

Figure 5.11 Boebot Grabbing the Book upon Receiving Signal from the Android app via Bluetooth.

Figure 5.12 Boebot Grabbing the Book and Taking it to theAppropriate Shelf.

Figure 5.13 Boebot Finally Places all the Books in their Appropriate Shelves.

5.7 Result and Discussion

The Test bed I has been tested for ten times and the results are summarized in Tables 5.1. and 5.2. The IR sensor for detecting books does not work all the time. Out of the ten runs, the robots could detect on 80% of the time. And only once out of ten trials, the android device could not establish connection with the robot giving a success rate of 90%. However, the overall success rate of 80% is achieved in putting the books at the appropriate shelf.

Table 5.1 The Number of Trials and the Success Rate.

Sl. No.	Trial number	Detect obstacle through IR sensor	Establish Connection with android	Could place the book at Shelf
1	1	Yes	Yes	Yes
2	2	Yes	Yes	Yes
3	3	Yes	No	No
4	4	Yes	Yes	Yes
5	5	No	Yes	No
6	6	Yes	Yes	Yes
7	7	Yes	Yes	No
8	8	Yes	Yes	Yes
9	9	No	Yes	Yes
10	10	Yes	Yes	Yes

The Table 5.2 shows the time taken for communication between robot-middleware and middleware-cloud. The communication between middle and robot is almost instantaneous because of the fact that it is less than one 1 second. Scanning the barcode takes approximately 1 minute. However, getting information from the cloud takes 3 seconds average owing to the internet connection used at that time

Table 5.2 The Number of Trials and the Time Taken for Communication.

Sl. No	Trial number	Time Taken to scan the barcode (in secs)	Time Taken to get the information from cloud (in secs)	Time taken to communicate with android interface and robot (in secs)
1	1	< 1	3	<1
2	2	< 1	4	< 1
3	3	< 1	3	< 1
4	4	1	5	< 1
5	5	1	3	< 1
6	6	1	4	< 1
7	7	2	3	< 1
8	8	1	2	< 1
9	9	1	3	< 1
10	10	1	3	< 1

5.8 Summary of the Chapter

Since the fixed length used is very less in size (less than 50 bytes), the time taken to transfer and get the result from the cloud (~1kbs) is fast. Such small strings can be used as a real time decision making aid when a robot needs information from the cloud database. Hence the use of variable string length in chapter 4 is validated.

Chapter 6

Robotic Framework for Variable Length String

6.1 Background

From the discussions in Chapter 4, it has now well understood that most often the robots used for knowledge sharing need not be homogeneous on account of their architecture and the programming languages, which makes it mandatory that the robots share a common type of representation. In such cases of heterogeneous robot communication, Knowledge Interchange Format (KIF) can play a major role for exchange of knowledge between different systems due to its ability of interchange of knowledge among disparate computer programs. While reading a knowledge base in KIF, a program converts and computes the data in its own internal form and then to communicate with another program it maps the internal data structures into KIF. Thus KIF enables practical means of translating declarative knowledge bases to and from typical knowledge representation languages.

In this Chapter, an attempt has been made to implement a length string to interchange knowledge between heterogeneous robots. The variable knowledge interchange format is the alphanumeric string which represents a path taken by a robot as discussed in Chapter 4. The regenerated string is stored in a server's shared memory. The robot, with different hardware configuration, accesses the shared memory and retrieves the string. The architecture is illustrated with a case study of "Robotic Framework for Variable Length String" for robot communication with a middleware and server and illustrated as Test bed II in the following sections.

6.2 Architecture of Test Bed II

Figure 6.1 depicts the architecture of Test bed II, consisting of a server and Personal Computers (PCs) serving as a client middleware platform. The middleware acts as an interface for communication between robots and servers.

In the initial design a server is created and a client machine is connected to it. The server hosts a site that contains the string i.e., the command for the robot to do a specific task. The client server retrieves the string and processes it. The string (chapter 4) is then sent to the robot that operates according to the string and returns a response. The client on receiving the response forwards it to the server. This generated response is the knowledge base or the intelligence that the robot has acquired during its navigation in the external environment. When some other robot is sent to the same environment, instead of trying to obtain its own knowledge, the robot is fed with the intelligence of the previous robot.

While designing, utmost care has also been taken to fix the following issues.

- Since the architecture and the language support of robots vary, the maps are represented in a common method understandable to all the robots by using the generalized length string.
- Communication between robots of different families has been achieved by employing an intermediate computer.
- Necessary measures are taken for the robots to keep track of the voltage level coming from the power supply.
- The friction coefficients of the surface on which the robot is running has been kept uniform to avoid the robot to deviate from its path.
- The anticipated problems due to variation in geometry of the wheels are taken care of by measuring the circumference of the wheel and by keeping constant voltage from the power supply.
- Open loop control system to be used in this test to validate/check/verify the proposed algorithm.

The server and the client can communicate between them either by using an Ad-hoc network or by using wired connection. Both these cases are found to be fairly satisfactory. The communication and transfer of data between the client and the robots can also be performed using a wired Universal Serial Bus (USB) medium or a Bluetooth medium.

6.3 Platform

Both the Software as well as the Hardware platforms used for the said architecture is described below.

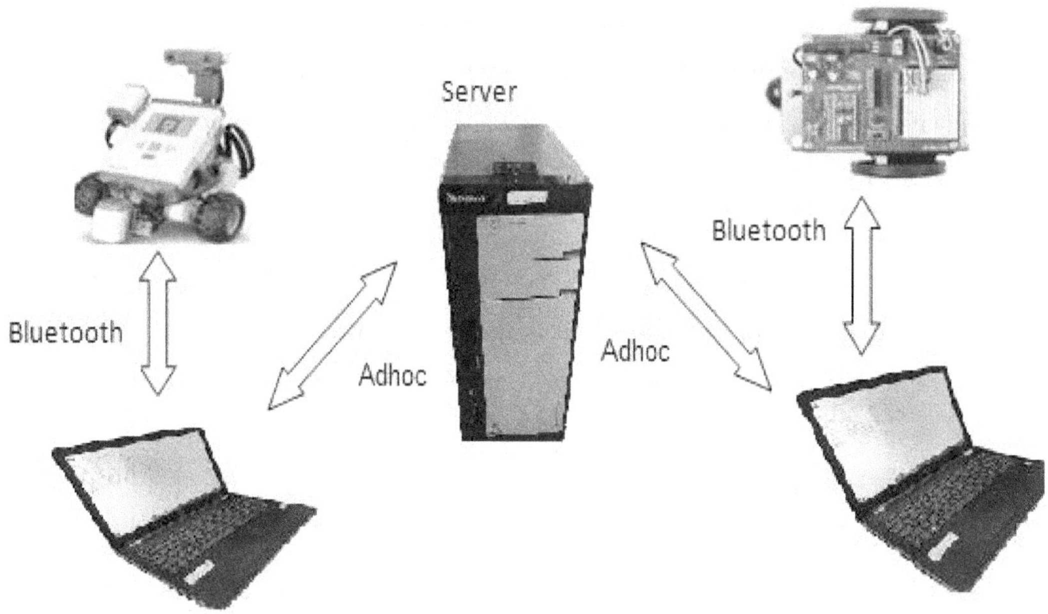

Figure 6.1: The Architecture of Robotic Framework for Variable Length String.

6.3.1 Software Platform

The requirement and Specifications for Software platform are listed below.

- Operating System: Microsoft ® Windows 7 or above, Android
- Language/Platforms: Pbasic using Basic Stamp (Boebot),
- NBC using Bricx Command Centre (Lego),
- Matlab 2012a (Windows).
- Microsoft Visual Studio 2010,
- Eclipse

6.3.2 Hardware Platform

The hardware requirements are summarized hereunder.

6.3.2.1 Lego MindstormNxt[97]

- Main processor: 32-bit ARM processor
  - 256 Kilo Byte FLASH Memory
  - 64 Kilo Byte RAM
  - 48 MHz
- Co-processor: 8-bit AVR processor
  - 4 Kilo Byte FLASH Memory
  - 512 Byte RAM
  - 8 MHz
- Bluetooth : CSR BlueCore
  - SPP support
  - 47 KByte RAM
  - 8 MBit FLASH
  - 26 MHz
  - USB port
- Display: LCD
  - 26 x 40.6 mm
- Speaker:
  - 2-16 KHz
- 4 button user-interface
- Power : 6 AA batteries
  - Alkaline batteries is recommend
  - Rechargeable Lithium-Ion battery 1400 mAH
- Connector: 6-wire

6.3.2.2 Parallax Boebot

- Microcontroller: Microchip PIC16C57c
- Ram Size: 32 bytes for BoeBot, 2 Gb of the computer
- Processor Size: 20MHz for BoeBot, 2.10 GHz of the computer

6.4 Setting up of Test Bed II

The setting up of Test Bed II comprises the setting up of (i) Laptop PC, (ii) Bricx Command Center, (iii) Basic Stamp (Parallax) and (iv) Matlab, each of which is explained below.

6.4.1 Setting up of Virtual Machine

Two virtual machines are created above the host operating system to serve as middleware. The host operating system acts as a server. One of the virtual machines is the interface between the host (server) and the Boebot. The other virtual machine is the interface between Lego Mindstorms NXT and server.

Bluetooth is used for message passing between the robots and the computer serving as a guest operating system. Ad-hoc is used to establish connection between computer or the guest operating system and the server.

6.4.2 Steps for Setting up Bricx Command Center

Lego mindstorm is programmed using bricx command center [97]. At the initiation of the program, it asks for the location of the robot. Most likely, the program will automatically find the robot. The user interface is described as "Bricx Command Center for Lego Mindstorm NXT"as shown in Figure 6.2.

The interface looks like a standard text editor, with the usual menus and buttons for common operations *viz;* 'to open and save files', 'print files', 'edit files' etc. But there are also some additional menus for special operations like compiling and downloading programs to the robot and for getting information from the robot.

Once the program is written, it is then compiled to change into binary codes to be understandable and executable by the robot. The compiled codes are then sent to the robot using Universal Serial Bus (USB) cable or Bluetooth (BT) dongle. This process can be termed as "downloading" the program.

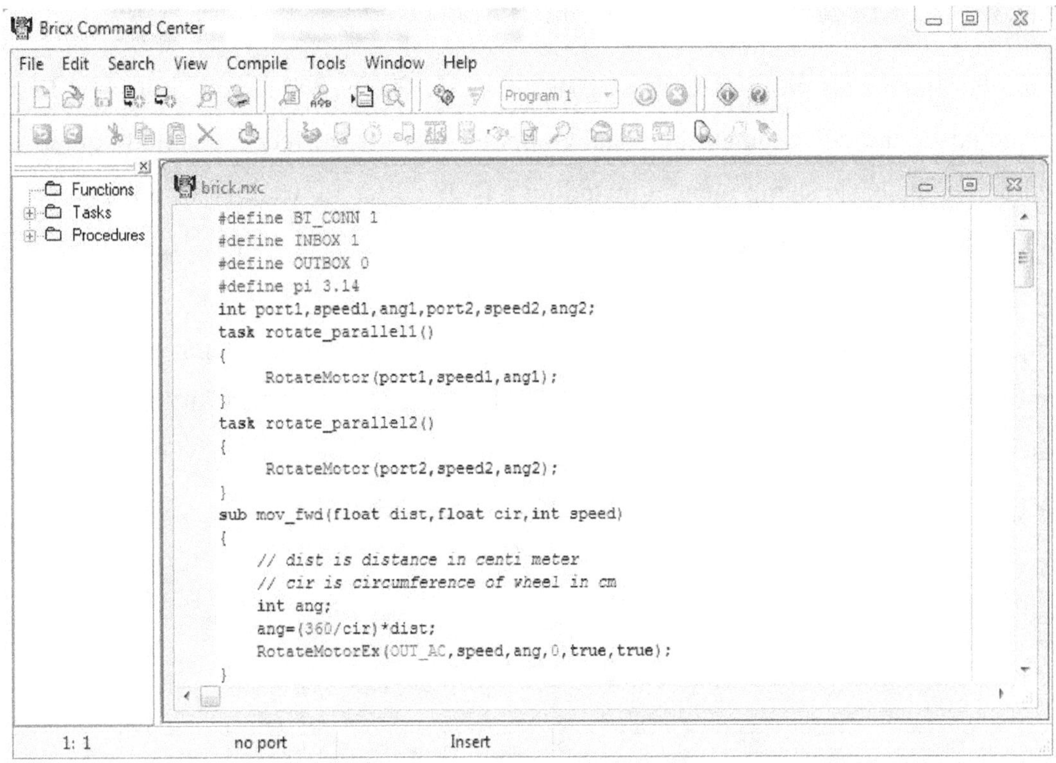

Figure 6.2 Bricx Command Center for Lego Mindstorm Nxt.

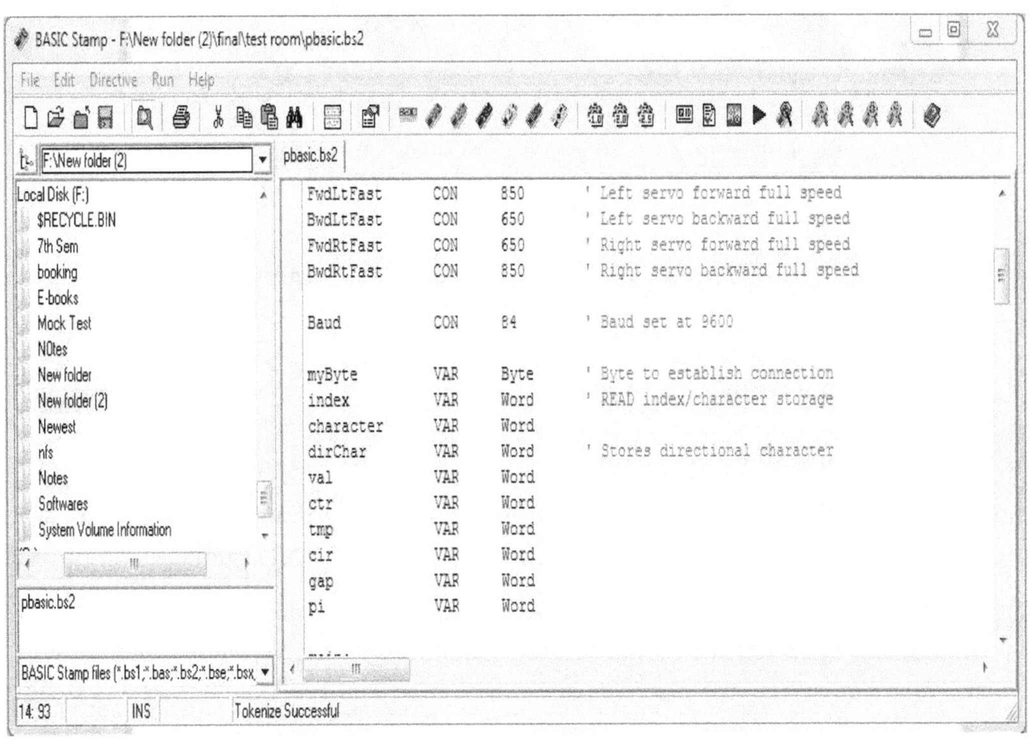

Figure 6.3 Basic Stamp (Parallax) Editor for Boebot.

6.4.3 Steps for Setting Basic Stamp (Parallax)

Parallax Boebot is programmed using pbasic [28]. The basic stamp editor must first be installed on the development personal computer. Parallax offers a detailed "quick start guide" in the basic stamp manual including a DOS editor for each type of basic stamp 2 and a single windows editor for all types of basic stamp 2 as shown in Figure 6.3.

Figure 6.4 shows the communication between the Basic Stamp 24 pin microcontroller and the debug window for the test program. The large part in black in the lower half of the debug window shows all of debugging output while the smaller white box above it acts as an input line for those characters expected from the robot.

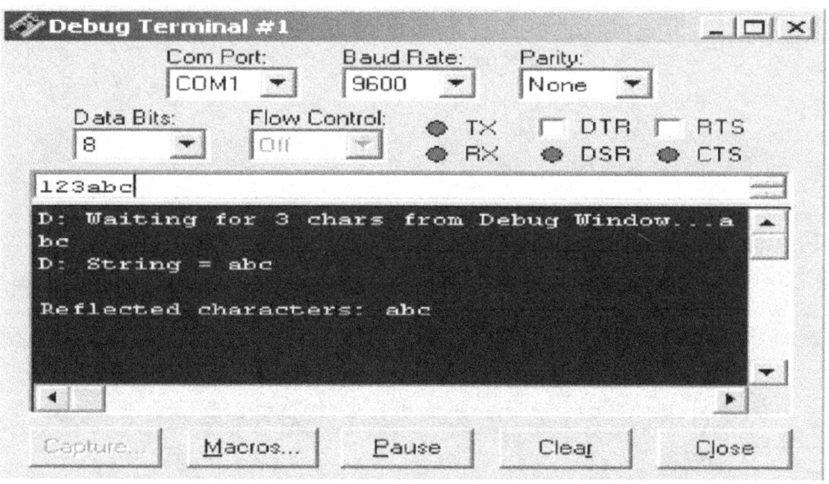

Figure 6.4Debugging Window Basic Stamp.

6.4.4 Steps for Setting up Matlab

The Bluetooth connection and the transfer of the required command to the respective robot is done with the help of Matlab. Figure 6.5 is the screenshot of the Matlab interface with the code written to transfer command i.e. the required string to the Lego mindstorm nxt.

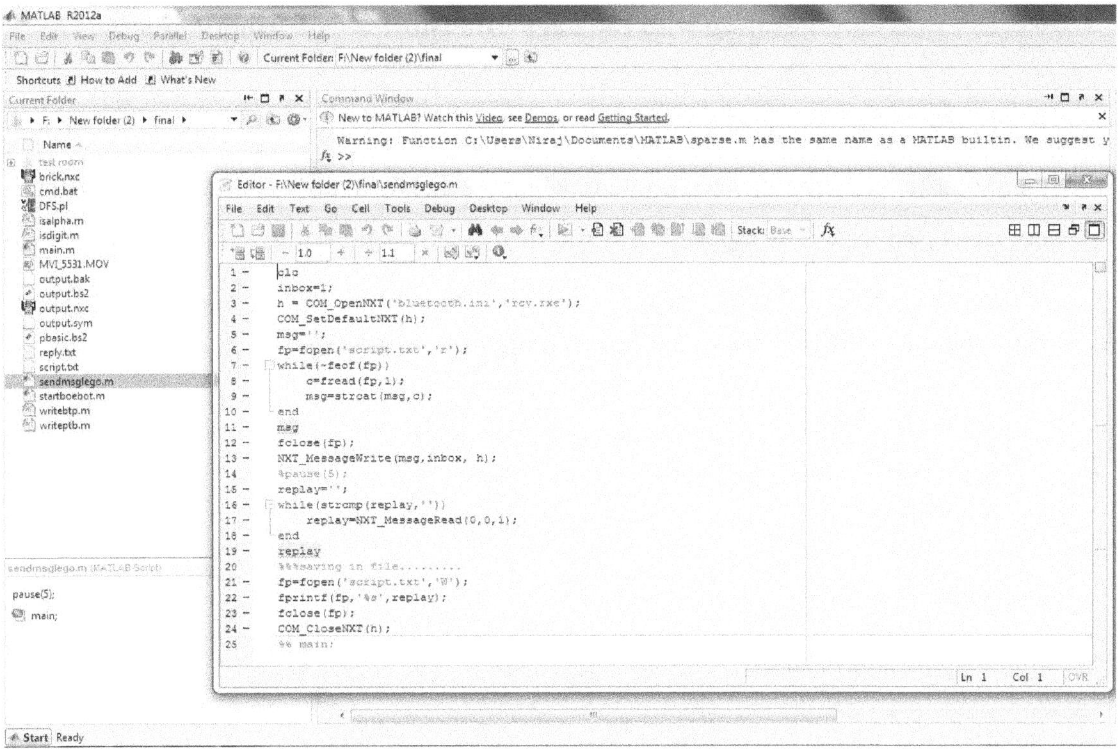

Figure 6.5 The Matlab Interface.

6.5 Implementation

The Flowchart of communication between computer and robot is shown in Figure 6.10. The computer opens a file containing the string and reads the file until the end of file (EOF) is reached and then sends the string file to the robot. On receipt of the string, the robot will start driving the wheel motors until the stop instruction (S) is found. The algorithms for Lego modules and Boebot are given in *section 6.5.4* and *section 6.5.5* respectively. The pseudo code of all the modules are given in *appendix vii* as "*Pseudo Code for Module inside Lego Mindstorm (Test Bed II)*" , *appendix viii* as "*Pseudo Code for Module Inside Parallax Boebot (Test Bed II)*" , *appendix ix* as "*Pseudo Code of Boebot for Sending Message*" and *appendix x* as "*Pseudo code of Lego Mindstorm for Sending Message*".

6.5.1 Communicating with the Lego Mindstorm NXT using Matlab

Before setting up a connection in Matlab, the Lego brick has to be paired with the client computer to make the device visible to Matlab[16].The list of all the available Bluetooth devices used can be obtained by initiating the instrhwinfo command. The"friendly" names of the Bluetooth devices can be made available by using the *RemoteNames* field from the output *ofinstrhwinfo* as shown in Figure 6.6 and Figure 6.7.

```
bluetoothDevices = instrhwinfo('Bluetooth')

remoteNames = bluetoothDevices.RemoteNames
```

```
bluetoothDevices =

        RemoteNames: {'NXT'}
          RemoteIDs: {'btspp://00165310E7C4'}
    BluecoveVersion: 'BlueCove-2.1.1-SNAPSHOT'
     JarFileVersion: 'Version 3.2'


remoteNames =

    'NXT'
```

Figure 6.6 Establishing Connectionwith NxtBrick from Matlab.

```
deviceInfo = instrhwinfo('Bluetooth','NXT')
```

```
deviceInfo =

               RemoteName: 'NXT'
                 RemoteID: 'btspp://00165310E7C4'
    ObjectConstructorName: {'Bluetooth('NXT', 1);'}
                 Channels: {'1'}
```

Figure 6.7 Establishing Connection with Matlab from NxtBrick.

6.5.2 Bluetooth Message Format

The format of the Bluetooth message is given in Figure 6.8. A Bluetooth message needs to have two byte in the front of the message itself to indicate how many bytes the message includes. The length of the packet is counted without the two length bytes.

Length, LSB	Length, MSB	Command Type	Command	Byte 5	Byte 6	

Figure 6.8 Bluetooth Message Format.

It specifies that to get the device information, the command should have following format:[97]

- Bytes 1:2 –" Length of command" = 2
- Byte 3 –"Type of command" = 1 ("since it is a system command with reply from device")

- Byte 4 –"Additional information to execute the command. Using this information, raw data packet is formed which is sent to the NXT brick"- 0x9B ("This value is defined by the Lego Mindstorms nxt communication protocol")

This means the raw data packet will be [2 0 1 155]. The first two no's 2 and 0 indicate that the length of the command is 2, the third byte location, 1, is a system command and 115 is the decimal equivalent of 0x9B.

Now this data is written to the brick.

The device then gives a response containing device information in the following format [97].

- Bytes 1:2 –"Length of response"
- Byte 3 –"Type of command issued"
- Byte 4 –"Data sent to device"
- Byte 5 –"Command status"
- Bytes 6:20 –"Name of device"
- Bytes 21:27 –"Bluetooth address"
- Byte 28 –"LSB of Bluetooth signal strength"
- Byte 29 –"Not defined"

- Byte 30 –“Not defined”
- Byte 31 –“MSB of Bluetooth signal strength”
- Byte 32 –“LSB of user flash”
- Byte 33 –“Not defined”
- Byte 34 –“Not defined”
- Byte 35 –“MSB of user flash”

The response from the brick is then read to get its information in the format as given in Figure 6.9.

```
btResponse = fread(bt,32)'
```

```
btResponse =

  Columns 1 through 13

    33     0     2   155     0    78    88    84     0     0     0     0
0

  Columns 14 through 26

     0     0     0     0     0     0     0     0    22    83    16   231
196

  Columns 27 through 32

     0     0     0     0     0   132
```

Figure 6.9 Responses from Brick.

The response from the Legobrick is obtained in the following format [23].

- Bytes 1:2 –“ Length of response” = 33
- Byte 3 –“Type of command issued” = 2
- Byte 4 –“Data sent to device” = 0x9B
- Byte 5 –“Command status” = 0 (if successful)
- Bytes 6:20 –“Name of device”
- Bytes 21:27 –“Bluetooth address”
- Byte 28 –“LSB of Bluetooth signal strength” = 0
- Byte 29 –“Not defined” = 0
- Byte 30 –“Not defined” = 0
- Byte 31 –“MSB of Bluetooth signal strength” = 0
- Byte 32 –“LSB of user flash” = 0
- Byte 33 –“Not defined” = 0

- Byte 34 –"Not defined" = 0
- Byte 35 –"MSB of user flash" = 132

To read only the name of the brick from its response, we know that the bytes 6 to 20 correspond to the brick's name.

6.5.3 Communicating with the Parallax Boebot using Matlab

To open the Bluetooth communication port of the Boebot, the EasyBT module is used with the following code.

bt= Bluetooth('EasyBT',1);

fpoen(bt);

The data to be sent to the Boebot is done as follows :

fwrite(bt,c);

where c is the byte to be sent.

After the data has been written on the Boebot the connection is closed using

close(bt);

6.5.4 Algorithm for Lego

Step 1: Start

Step 2: Receive string when ReceiveRemoteString is true

Step 3: Store the string in 'A' array

Step 4: If A[i] is equal to 'L", turn Left

Step 5: Else if A[i] is equal to 'R', turn Right

Step 6: Else if A[i] is equal to 'F', calculate distance and move forward

Step 7: Else if A[i] is equal to 'B', turn 180 degree, calculate distance and move forward

Step 8 : Else if A[i] 'S" , goto step 10.

Step 9 : Goto step 2 until the array is empty

Step 10: Stop

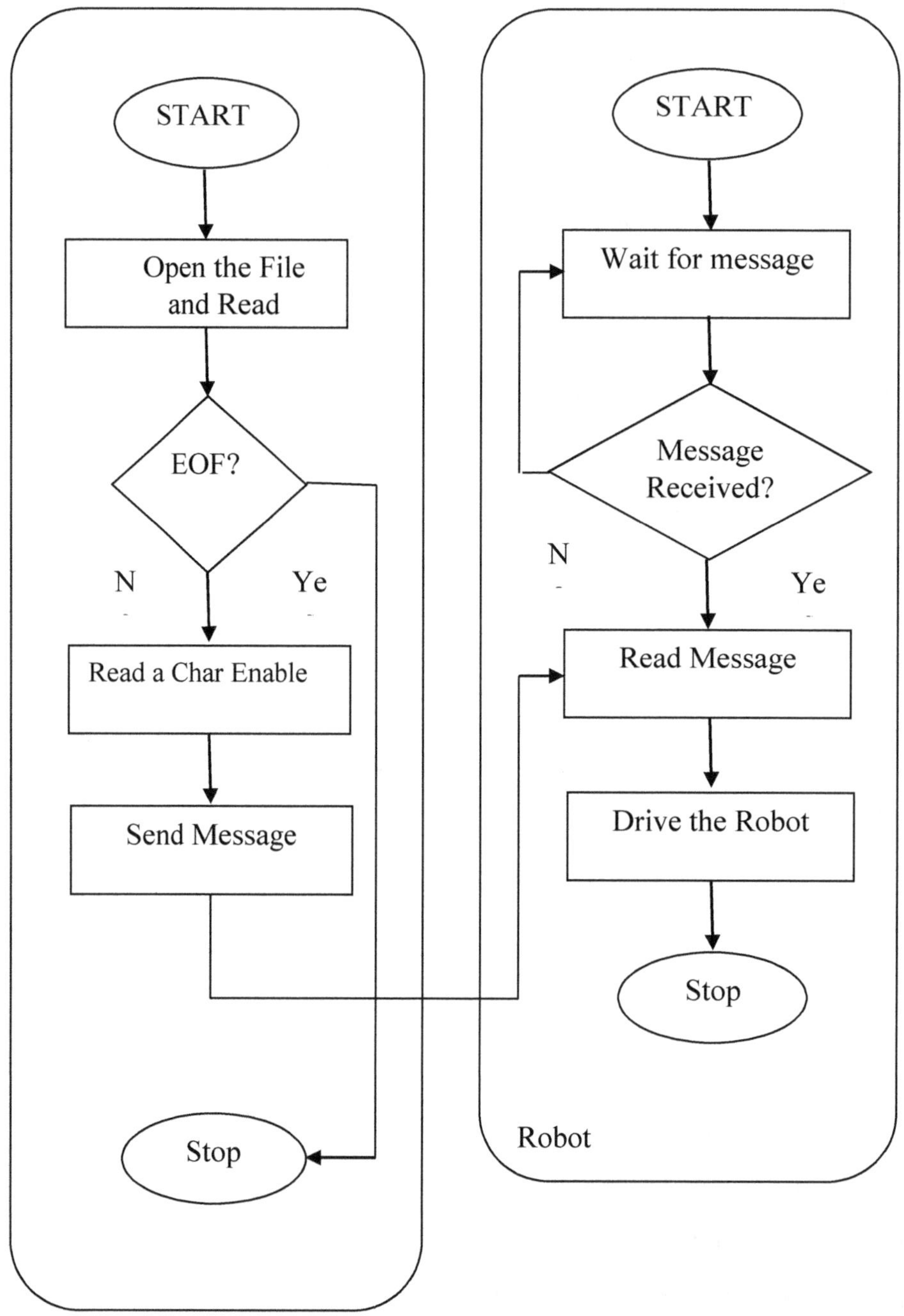

Figure 6.10 Flowchart of Communication between Computer and Robot.

6.5.5 Algorithm for Boebot

Step 1: Start

Step 2: Receive string when ReceiveRemoteString is true

Step 3: Store the string in 'B' array

Step 4: If B[i] is equal to ‘L”, turn Left

Step 5: Else if B[i] is equal to ‘R’, turn Right

Step 6: Else if B[i] is equal to ‘F’, calculate distance and move forward

Step 7: Else if B[i] is equal to ‘B’, turn 180 degree, calculate distance and move forward

Step 8 : Else if B[i] ‘S” , goto step 10.

Step 9 : Goto step 2 until the array is empty

Step 10: Stop

Table 6.1TimeTaken for Communication Between Modules.

Sl. No	Trial number	Time Taken for boebot - server communication (in secs)	Time Taken for Lego - server communication	Time Taken to get the information from Virtual server (in secs)
1	1	<1	<1	<1
2	2	<1	<1	<1
3	3	<1	<1	<1
4	4	<1	<1	<1
5	5	<1	<1	<1
6	6	<1	<1	<1
7	7	<1	<1	<1
8	8	<1	<1	<1
9	9	<1	<1	<1
10	10	<1	<1	<1

6.6 Results and Discussion

The test bed 2 has been tested for ten times and the result is given in table 6.1. Since the experiment is done in simulated environment, the time taken for communication between all the modules takes less than 1 second. Considering the robots used in the test bed are educational/ research robots and not industrial grade robots, so 1s is considered fair. Out of the ten trials, the robots could reach the designated goal successfully with very less time.

Both Boebot and Lego could follow a same path using the variable string even though they have different platforms.

6.7 Summary of the Chapter

The test bed 2 is tested successfully and the following points are observed:

- The latency time taken to communicate with the server and robots are fast (less than 1 sec)
- The variable string is suitable for sharing and real time decision making aids when the robot needs information from the cloud database.

Chapter 7

Cloud-Enabled Robotic Framework using Landmark and Variable Length String

7.1 Background

Many studies have been undertaken by the researchers to develop various techniques and principles regarding the Navigation of robots using landmarks. In landmark identification and navigation of robots, vision has been considered a major element. Hayet et.al[35] has studied the visual landmark framework for mobile robot navigation based on natural visual landmarks using the concept of SLAM paradigm. Though the proposed system is found to be invariant to the lightning conditions but the use of SLAM does not prove effective as it could be CPU intensive and additional task is not allowed. Zhang et.al [123] has used the artificial landmark*viz;* 2D barcode based on computer vision. In this approach the system creates a map for the indoor environment and allows robots to navigate. Even if the use of artificial markers makes the navigation faster and efficient, it fails to make use of movement orientation during the robot navigation. Zainuddin et.al [123] proposed a system to navigate using a kinect sensor, which acquires a video and converts it into 3D point cluster using clustering and filtration process. However, the drawbacks of the system are that the quality of image captured is poor and the landmark may be misidentified due to presence of large outliers especially in large environments. Lee et.al [63], presented an autonomous tour guide robot by using ultrasonic range sensors and Quick Response (QR) code recognition in indoor environment for navigation using cloud. The introduction of cloud with robotics reduced the overhead caused on the robot and improved performance and computational skill. Data fusion with an advanced sensing system for automated guided vehicles has been proposed. But the major limitation is to make the robot navigate freely by increasing the flexibility and also in classifying the object.

Limosani et.al [67] has attempted to enable global robot navigation based on a cloud robotics approach. It aims to provide navigation in a complex environment by making use of environmental tags with cloud Software as a Service (SaaS) and map supervisor for navigation of mobile robots. The Augmented Reality (AR) tag and QRtag is used as environmental tags to provide information about the remote resource. The system proposed makes use of artificial landmarks and is not based on recognition of the scene.

In this chapter, an attempt has been made to generate the common representation for paths for the robot to navigate in an unknown environment on a cloud based architecture and natural landmarks. The navigation is made by detecting and identifying landmarks using scene recognition technique. Landmark refers to an object placed between the range of the camera used in the test bed. The robot in this scenario identifies a landmark with the help of machine learning technique applied by Google cloud and simultaneously generates a path map. It then shares the path map with different robots after it has been processed. The other robot needs to localize itself relative to the map provided. Localization means position estimation and position control. This can be achieved by using a probabilistic framework of Markov localization to maintain a position probability density over a whole set of possible robot poses. Markov localization can also deal with ambiguous situations and re-localize the robot in the case of localization failures. The system architecture of Cloud enabled Robotic framework using Landmark and Variable Length String is illustrated as Test bed III in the following section.

7. 2 System Architecture of Test Bed III

The system architecture of Test bed III for the navigation of cloud enabled robots using a natural landmark is shown in the Figure 7.1 below.

The module begins with cloud communication using gateway or middleware. The sensor is used to detect the landmark ahead of the robot which, when sensed, is then captured by camera and uploaded to cloud in jpeg format. Using the Google cloud services the landmark is then identified and navigation proceeds creating a map which is stored in the cloud. This information can be shared with other robots so as to enable them to follow the path. The block diagram in Figure 7.2 below depicts the different states the system undergoes. The data dictionary for the states is as below.

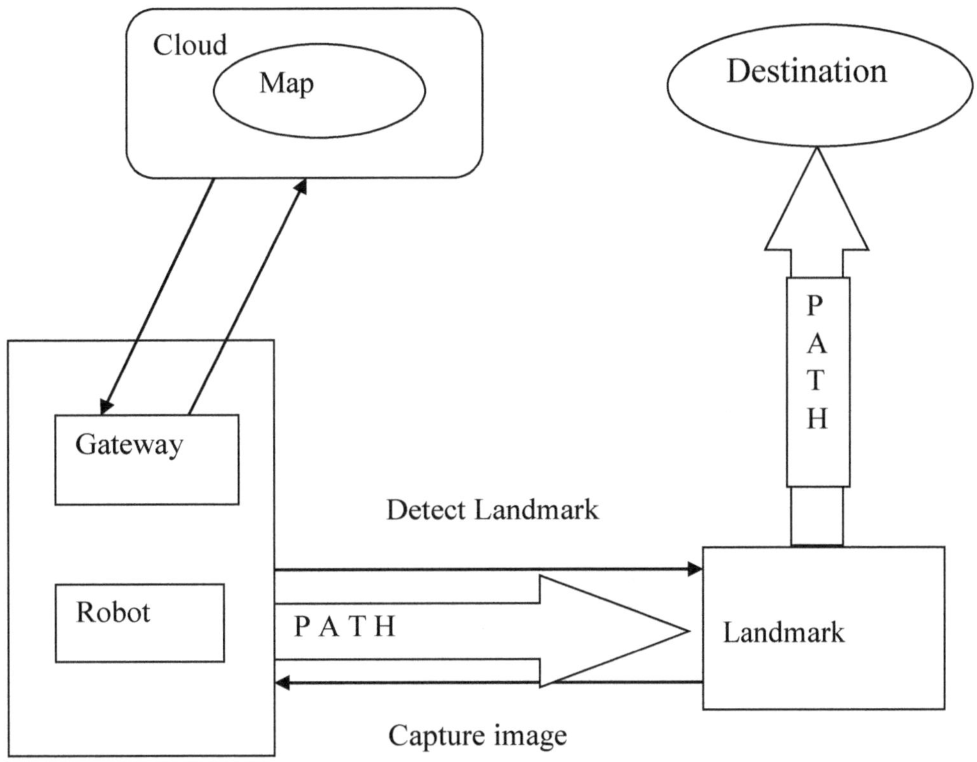

Figure 7.1 Architectural Diagram of Cloud Robot Navigation Based on Landmark.

1. Ultrasonic sensor: if distance of 40cm to 70cm HALT robot.
2. Image capture: image.jpg
3. Request for service: Google application credential creation as robot1.json; encode and upload image.jpg.
4. Response: Description; longitude; latitude. x coordinate; y coordinate of image.jpg
5. Map upload: firstmap.txt(20L15R10S)
6. Navigate: forward( );left( );right( );stop( );backward( )

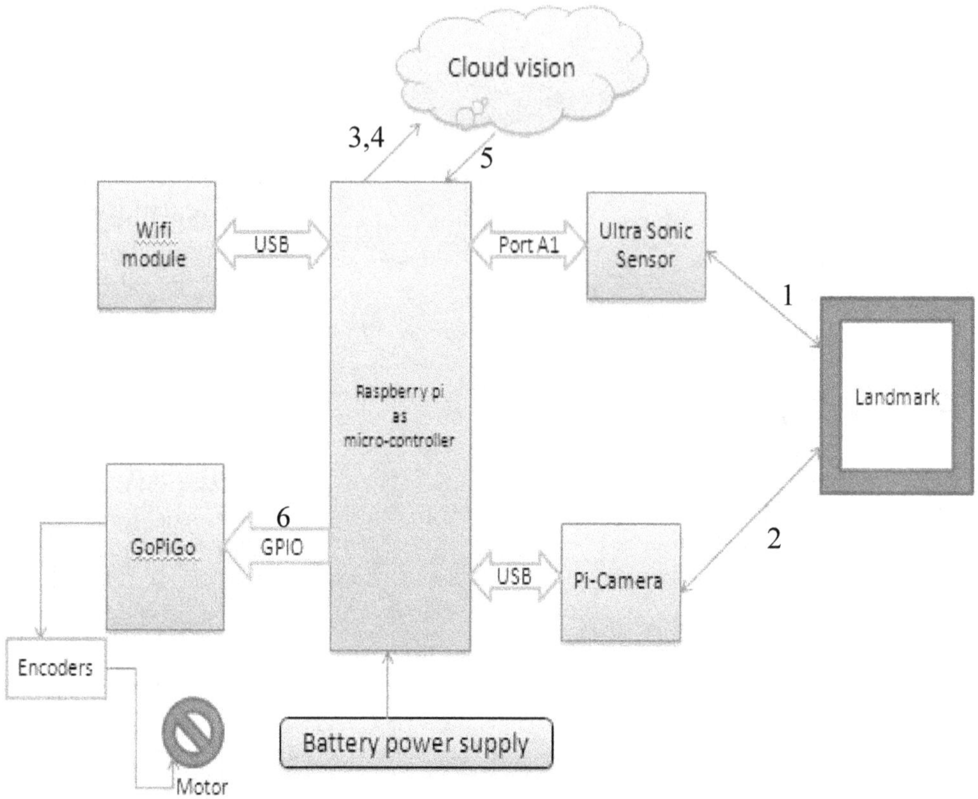

Figure 7.2 Block Diagram.

In the present study, a Raspberry Pi controller is used as the master robot that controls the robotic movement with the help of computers or smartphones. It autonomously navigates on identifying the landmark until the destination is reached. The identification and decision making is based on the application provided by Google cloud. The Raspberry Pi controller is coupled with GoPiGo motor control board that drives the motor on the decision provided from the raspberry pi using the service provided by cloud. Raspberry pi makes an interface to the cloud so as to access and monitor the information required for robot navigation through the use of Wi-Fi modules.

The purpose of developing the system is to achieve the target that can provide following functionality in terms of five various modules:

1. To activate a gateway that provides an interface to control GoPiGo which involves forward, backward, left, right and stop navigation system.

2. GoPiGo detects landmarks by using distance measurement sensors such as ultrasonic sensors.
3. GoPiGo to capture real time images of landmarks using a pi camera when a landmark is detected using an ultrasonic sensor.
4. Create connectivity between cloud and robot and request for landmark identification in the image captured so as they navigate accordingly.
5. To generate a path map on the process of navigation.

The flow of control for the system is also shown in the Figure 7.4 below.

7.3 Tools Used

The tools used are briefly divided into hardware and software.

7.3.1 Hardware Components Used

These include various hardware components used in the test bed III.

7.3.1.1 Raspberry Pi 3 model B

The third generation Raspberry Pi 3 model B made of the latest Broadcom 2837 ARMv8 64bit processor is shown in Figure 7.3. Processor speed ranges from 700 MHz to 1.2 GHz for the Pi 3 and on board memory range from 256 MB to 1 GB RAM and is faster and more powerful than its predecessors. On account of its built-in wireless and Bluetooth connectivity it becomes the perfect IoT ready solution [43].

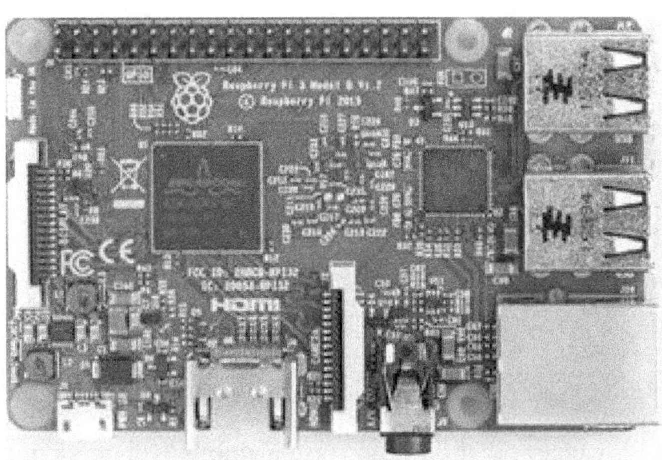

Figure 7.3 Raspberry Pi 3 ModelB. (Courtesy: in.element14.com)

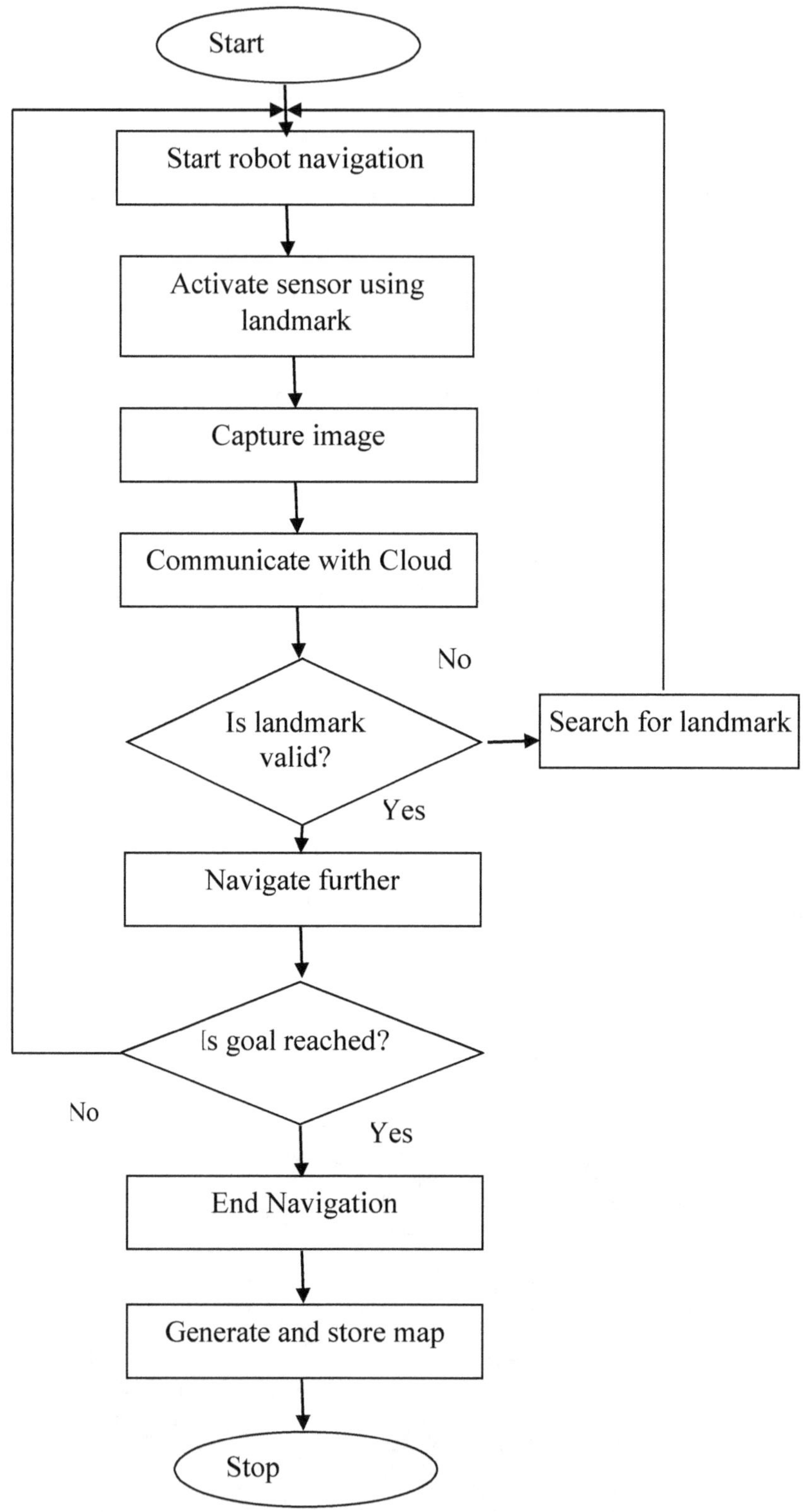

Figure 7.4 Flowchart for the Cloud Based Mobile Robot Navigation.

7.3.1.2 Power Supply

The Raspberry Pi 3 is powered by a +5.1V micro USB supply. The exact current (mA) requirement of the Raspberry Pi depends on what is being connected to it. It has been observed that a 2.5A power supply is sufficient to run the Raspberry Pi [20].

7.3.1.3 Raspberry Pi Camera

The Raspberry Pi Camera Module v2 is a high quality 8 megapixel Sony IMX219 image sensor custom designed add-on board for Raspberry Pi, having a fixed focus lens [43]. The main features of the camera are listed below.

"Second Generation Raspberry Pi Camera Module with Fixed Focus Lens
Sony Exmor IMX219 Sensor Capable of 4K30, 1080P60, 720P180, 8MP Still
3280 x 2464 (V) Active Pixel Count
3281 Maximum of 1080P30 and 8MP Stills in Raspberry Pi Board
2A Power Supply Highly Recommended"

7.3.1.4 Ultrasonic Sensor

Ultrasonic ranging module HC - SR04 consisting of ultrasonic transmitters, receiver and control circuit as shown in Figure 7.5 provides 2cm - 400cm non-contact measurement function with a ranging accuracy of 3mm. The basic working principle [39] is detailed below.

The Module detects a pulse signal back by sending eight 40 kHz automatically using IO trigger for at least 10us high level signal. If the signal back through high level, then the time of high output IO duration is taken as the time from sending ultrasonic to returning. The distance is then calculated as:

distance = (high level time × velocity of sound (340M/S) / 2.

Figure 7.5 Ultrasonic Sensor (Courtesy: controllerstech.com)

7.3.1.5 GopiGo Board

The brain of the GoPiGo board as shown in Figure 7.6 below is an ATMEGA328 microcontroller part 8 with built-in 32KB flash memory and 2KB SRAM (static random-access memory) to help the CPU retrieve commands faster [111]. The features are:

- Serial interface
- 23 GPIOS and
- SPI serial port
- Servo Header, Raspberry Pi Header and ISP Header.
- Optical Encoders
- Microcontroller
- Raspberry Pi prototyping pins
- TB6612FNG motor controller

Figure 7.6 GoPiGo Board.

The GoPiGo board is compatible with computer hardware and software. The Raspberry Pi fits well on top of the GoPiGo board and connects each other via I2C interface to communicate commands to the GoPiGo brain (the ATMEGA328 microcontroller) [111]. The GoPiGo board embedded with three headers *viz;* Servo Header, Raspberry Pi Header and ISP Headeralso features Raspberry Pi prototyping pins, Level Conversion chip and TB6612FNG motor controller to control two DC motors independently. The sensors like temperature, accelerometer and GPS can be connected to the several analog and digital ports available on the GoPiGo board. The microcontroller, as well as two Optical Encoders with 18 pulse counts per rotation,on the back of the board helps it to move precisely in a straight line. A pack of eight 1.5V batteries is sufficient to power the motors, ultrasonic sensor, servo and Raspberry, as the board can operate with 7V - 12V voltage [111].

7.3.2 Software Requirement

These include various software components used in the testbed III.

7.3.2.1 Raspbian for Robots SD Card

The Raspberry Pi primarily uses Raspbian, a Debian-based Linux operating system. Though many other operating systems can also run on the Raspberry Pi, the present study makes use of Raspbian Jessie release.

7.3.2.2 Cloud Service Account

The cloud vision provided by Google has been used for the present study. The steps followed to connect GoPiGo with the cloud are stated as follows.

- Create an account in Google cloud console
- Create a new project. Project id is created.
- Provide billing details
- Select API manager and select the created project
- Create credentials for the selected project and generate a service key.
- Download js on file into the local system for it to use for connectivity.

7.3.2.3 Python 2 .7.3 IDLE

Python, a powerful language capable of giving instant results has been implemented in the IDLE environment. Its name is an acronym of "Integrated Development Environment". The Python syntax is easy to visualize. It works well on both UNIX and Windows platforms. It has a Python shells window, which gives access to the Python interactive mode. It also has a file editor that creates and edits existing Python source files.

7.4 Implementation

This section describes the working of different modules for testbed III using various interfaces.

7.4.1 System Interfaces, Inputs and Outputs

This section consists of system interfaces used and their inputs and outputs.

7.4.1.1 System Interfaces

The system interface consists of entities such as GoPiGo robot provided by Dexter Industries, Raspberry Pi 3 model B, Ultrasonic sensor, Raspberry Pi camera module, Wi-Fi module and DC Motor. The robot with raspberry pi 3 acts as the base hardware, which is the gateway that connects to the cloud. The cloud service used is the Google cloud vision, which provides a REST API that has an analytical capability to identify and detect natural landmarks in the image captured by the raspberry pi camera. The DC motor driven by the GoPiGo driver is also in synchronization with the raspberry pi which makes the robot perform the required kinds of motion. The prerequisites for the system to work are:

- Wi-Fi module to be connected to raspberry Pi model B.
- Internet connectivity to be maintained in the robot.
- Google cloud project to be enabled.

7.4.1.2 Inputs/Outputs

The Image in jpg format captured from raspberry pi camera module acts as an input to Google cloud using service key in the form of json file created for the specified project. Two distinct outputs generated during the process are

- Cloud performs analysis of the image received and detects landmarks and sends the output to the robot enabling GoPiGo to navigate further based on the decision made.

- Simultaneously generate a path map in the form of generalized variable length string such as 10L20RS, where '10' is the magnitude of distance traveled in terms of centimeter and 'L' means on the left of the present location of the robot. '20R' means the robot has travelled 20 centimeter on the right. Finally S means the robot has reached the destination.

7.4.2 Working Mechanisms

In the present study, the use of cloud vision services provides a mechanism to understand the content of an image by encapsulating powerful machine learning model with pre-trained models. The cloud service Google cloud vision used can analyze the real time images uploaded by the GoPiGo robot controlled by raspberry pi. Raspberry pi, the master robot, is used as a gateway between the robot and cloud. It uses ultrasonic sensors to determine distance from a robot to the nearest landmark and also to avoid obstacles in order to navigate. The problem that has been defined in this system is the sharing of knowledge acquired by the master robot to the follower robot. The system is also designed to demonstrate the use of different modes of communication. The system is developed to achieve the target that can provide following functionality in terms of the following five various modules.

1. To activate a gateway that provides an interface to control GoPiGo which involves forward, backward, left, right and stop navigation system.
2. GoPiGo detects landmarks by using distance measurement sensors such as ultrasonic sensors.

3. GoPiGo to capture real time images of landmarks using a pi camera when a landmark is detected using an ultrasonic sensor.
4. Create connectivity between cloud and robot and request for landmark identification in the image captured so as they navigate accordingly.
5. To generate a path map simultaneously during navigation.

The detailed description of each module is as given below.

7.4.2.1 Module 1

The main function is to activate the gateway that provides an interface to control the assembled GoPiGo as shown is Figure 7.7 below. It involves forward, backward, left, right and stop navigation systems. The following steps are followed.

(a) Assemble GoPiGo with motors and chassis.
(b) Prepare Raspberry Pi by setting up a SD card.
(c) Install the Raspbian software on SD card.
(d) Powering GoPiGo with 8XAA batteries.
(e) Connecting GoPiGo to activate the gateway by either using Wi-Fi or Ethernet cable.

Figure 7.7 AssembledGoPiGo Board.

7.4.2.2 Module 2

This module measures the distance detected by the Ultrasonic. The circuit diagram and the circuit connect of the modules are shown in Figures 7.8 (a) and (b) below.

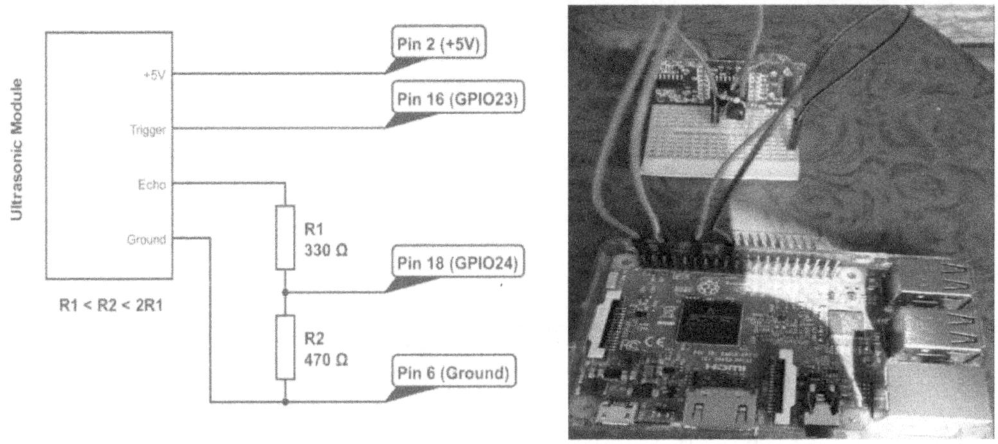

(a) Circuit Diagram (b) Circuit Connection

Figure 7.8 Ultrasonic Sensor Connection.

The codes to measure the distance using an Ultrasonic sensor are listed below.

Start function def measure():

```
GPIO.output(GPIO_TRIGGER, True)
time.sleep(0.00001)
GPIO.output(GPIO_TRIGGER, False)
start = time.time()
while GPIO.input(GPIO_ECHO)==0:
start = time.time()
while GPIO.input(GPIO_ECHO)==1:
stop = time.time()
elapsed = stop-start
distance = (elapsed * 34300)/2
return distance
def measure_average():
 # This function takes 3 measurements and
 # returns the average.
 distance1=measure()
time.sleep(0.1)
 distance2=measure()
time.sleep(0.1)
 distance3=measure()
distance = distance1 + distance2 + distance3
```

```
distance = distance / 3
return distance
GPIO.setmode(GPIO.BCM)
GPIO_TRIGGER = 23
GPIO_ECHO    = 24
print "Ultrasonic Distance Measurement"
GPIO.setup(GPIO_TRIGGER,GPIO.OUT)  # Trigger
GPIO.setup(GPIO_ECHO,GPIO.IN)      # Echo
GPIO.output(GPIO_TRIGGER, False)
while True:
distance = measure_average()
print distance
time.sleep(1)
```

7.4.2.3 Module 3

GoPiGo is deployed to capture real time images of landmarks when the ultrasonic sensor detects the landmark within a certain distance. The codes to capture images by pi-camera are as follows.

```
“From picamera import PiCamera
From time import sleep
Camera=PiCamera()
Camera.start_preview()
Sleep(5)
Camera,capture(‘home/pi/image.jpg’)
Camera.stop_preview()”
```

7.4.2.4 Module 4

It is used to create connectivity with the Google cloud and to integrate landmark detection code with GoPiGo when the real time image is uploaded to the cloud, mainly to make the GoPiGo navigate as LEFT, RIGHT, FORWARD, BACKWARD or STOP, based on the decision made. The Commands to prepare GoPiGo to connect with Cloud vision are listed below.

- Sudo pip install libjpeg8-dev
- Sudo pip install - - upgrade google-api-python-client
- Sudo pip install - - upgrade Pillow
- Sudo apt-get install python-picamera
- Sudo su
- Export GOOGLE_APPLICATION_CREDENTIALS=filename.json
- Run the program named as cloud-vision-landmark.py

The codes for landmark detection for the image that has been captured are written as follows.

```
BEGIN GoPiGo
   Forward()
   Sleep(1)
   Stop()
   Sleep(1)
Activate picamera
def takephoto():
  camera = picamera.PiCamera()
  camera.capture('image.jpg')
def main():
  Call takephoto()
"credentials = GoogleCredentials.get_application_default()
  service = discovery.build('vision', 'v1', credentials=credentials)
  with open('image.jpg', 'rb') as image:
    image_content = base64.b64encode(image.read())
    service_request = service.images().annotate(body={
      'requests': [{
        'image': {
          'content': image_content.decode('UTF-8')
        },
        'features': [{
          'type': 'LANDMARK_DETECTION',
          'maxResults': 10"
```

```
            }]
        }]
    })
    response = service_request.execute()
    print json.dumps(response, indent=4, sort_keys=True)
```

7.4.2.5 Module 5

Navigation process simultaneously generates a path map and is stored in the cloud. Any robot that wants to traverse the same path may do so by downloading it from the cloud. For safe and autonomous navigation of mobile robots in an unknown environment, the knowledge about one's position within its own environment is a precondition for making use of a map [25]. The path map generated by GoPiGo is in the form of the variable length string as discussed in Chapter 4.

7.5 Results and Discussion

An experimental study has been undertaken for the proposed system. For the master robot GoPiGo controlled by raspberry pi, a practical approach of determining the speed of the robot has been verified with the hardware configured motor and its actual movement. It also determines the range of the sensor at which the landmark would be detected and identified accurately.

7.5.1 Average Speed of Gopigo Robot

The average speed of GoPiGo robot is determined by making it undergo forward movement a number of times while giving various time periods for the motor movement as shown in Table 7.1. The average speed of the robot is then determined using two different methods, as stated below.

7.5.1.1 Method 1

The average speed taken by GoPiGo robot is calculated by taking the average of speed S of four different time periods as and is given as:

Average speed= (S1+S2+S3+S4)/4 (7.1)

The outcomes of the trial runs for different time periods are shown in Table 7.1 below. Using the Equation (7.1), the Average speed is calculated to be = (9.96+9.925+9.8+10.1)/4 = 9.946 cm/sec.

7.5.1.2 Method2

The average speed taken by GoPiGo can also be calculated on the basis of physical attributes such as wheel diameter of the robot and the number of rotations made etc., as detailed below. Accordingly, the average speed can be defined as:

Average speed (S) of robot = (No. of rotations of wheel for a time interval/ Duration of Time interval) (7.2)

For a single rotation, average speed = C/time taken for a complete rotation.

Table 7.1 Average Speed of GoPiGo.

Time T in Seconds	**No of trails (Distance D in cm)**				***Average distance* (cm)**	**S=D/T (cm /sec)**
	Trail 1	***Trail 2***	***Trial 3***	***Trial 4***	***D***	***Speed S***
20	200	199	200	198	199.25	9.96 (S1)
10	98	100	99	100	99.25	9.925 (S2)
5	50	48	48	50	49	9.8 (S3)
2.5	26	25	24	26	25.25	10.1 (S4)

Where C = Circumference of the wheel (Circle) = π x D

D= Diameter of the wheel of the robot.

Now, given values: Diameter (D) of wheel of robot=6 cm,

Circumference(C) of a circle= $\pi * D$ cm$=\frac{22}{7} * 6$ cm $= 18.85$ cm

Given the rotation per minute (rpm) of wheel of GoPiGo be 30 rpm, then considering that the wheel rotates 5 times in a time duration of 10 sec, we get 1 sec$=\frac{5}{10}$ rotation

Hence by using the Eqn (7.2), we get

Average speed (S) of GoPiGo $=\frac{5}{10}$ *18.85cm = 9.425 cm/sec

It can be observed from above that the average speed of GoPiGo from Method 1 is 9.946 and that from Method 2 is 9.425 and can be treated approximately as equal.

7.5.2 Accuracy Range for the Identification of Landmark

GoPiGo has been tested to identify the range of distance at which the ultrasonic sensor could detect the landmark and capture an image accurately. Table 7.2 and Figure 7.9 below show the accuracy of capturing an image of a landmark from a range of distance and identifying it. The results of % accuracy obtained in the last column of the Table 7.2 and the corresponding Figure 7.9 conclude that the accuracy in detecting landmarks is highest within the range of 41cm to 70 cm.

Table 7.2 Accuracy Range.

Sl. No	Ultrasonic distance range (cm)	Landmark identified out of 10	Accuracy in %
1	0-10	0	0
2	11-20	0	0
3	21-30	0	0
4	31-40	7	70
5	41-50	9	90
6	51-60	10	100
7	61-70	10	100
8	71-80	7	70
9	81-90	2	20

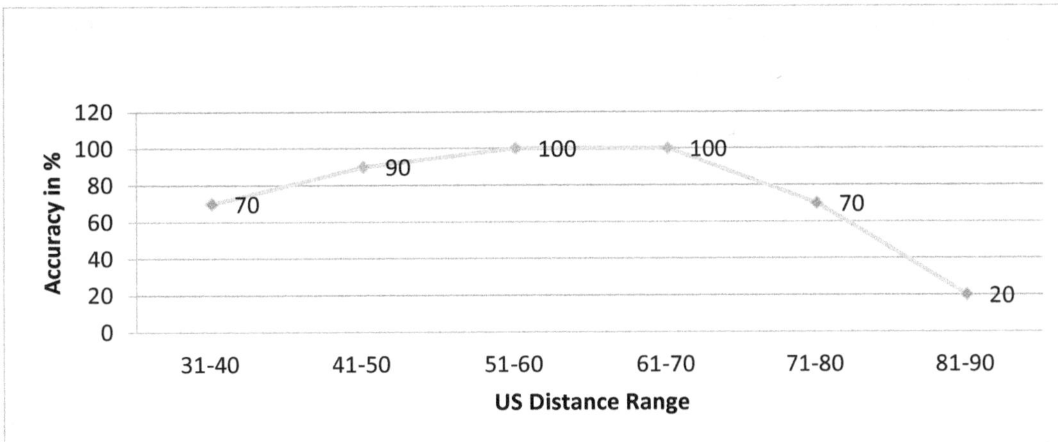

Figure 7.9 Graphs for Accuracy of Landmark Identification.

7.5.3 Calibration of Time for Follower Robot

As discussed above, the decision making for the follower robot is governed by the decision made by the master robot. Accordingly, the path generated by the master robot is requested by the follower robot to perform the course of action accordingly. It is not always possible that both the master robot and the follower robot need be homogeneous in nature. In the case of robots being heterogeneous in nature, it is most important that the path generated by the master robot needs to be in general form. In the present case, the path generated is therefore in the form of simple strings which include the time taken for the wheel of the robot to drive to the landmark and make a decision to navigate left (L) or to right(R) or forward (F) or stop (S) . The format of the path is 10L20R10FS.

Even with the general form of the path it is observed that since the wheel diameter of every robot may be different, the time taken by the master robot may not be the same for the follower robot. As the follower robot passes through an interface before it receives the path, it is essential that the interface is capable of masking the heterogeneity of the robots to enable the follower robot to follow the same path. Hence, every follower robot needs to be calibrated before beginning navigation. In this study, the calibration is done with reference to the difference in the wheel-diameter and the number of rotation the wheel of the robot takes in a second, as detailed below.

Considering a follower robot with wheel-diameter of 'x' cm and capable of 'y' rotation per second takes 'T2' seconds, we can calculate

Distance (D) in 1 rotation= $\pi * x$ cm (7.3) and

Distance (D) in 1 sec=$Y * \pi * x$ cm (7.4)

Hence considering the calculations in Section 7.5.1.1 and T1 as the time taken by master robot, we get

$$\frac{D}{9.946} = \frac{T2}{T1}$$

$$T2 = D * \frac{T1}{9.946} \quad (7.5)$$

From the above equation (7.5), it can be deduced the time taken for any robot based on the master robot. The findings state that any robot can be made to follow the master robot by calibrating the average speed based on the diameter of the wheel and the rotation of the wheel per minute.

7.5.4 Surface Area covered by Raspberry Pi Camera for Viewing

The experiment taken up determines the surface area covered by raspberry pi. The area is in the form of a trapezoid named ABCD as shown in Figure 7.11. This study provides information about obtaining the accurate landmark from the captured image increasing the performance of the system.

A mathematical calculation as per Figure 7.11 is performed in the following equation determining the surface area for a raspberry pi camera to view the image precisely and accurately.

By the similarity property of the trianglesΔ OAF and ΔODE in Figure 7.11, we get

$$\frac{AF}{OF} = \frac{DE}{OE} \quad (7.6)$$

$$DE = \frac{AF\ X\ OE}{OF} \quad (7.7)$$

$$= \frac{57.25\ X\ 48}{100} = \mathbf{27.48}$$

$$DC = 2 \text{ x } DE \quad (7.8)$$

$= 2$ x 27.48

$= 54.96$

In trapezoid ABCD

CD=54.96 cm

AB= 114.5 cm

EF=52

Therefore, the area of trapezoid

$$ABCD=\frac{1}{2}EF(AB + CD) \qquad (7.9)$$

$$= 4405.96 \text{ cm}^2$$

Accordingly, the static area covered by the raspberry pi camera of GoPiGo robot at particular instance is 4405.96 cm^2.

Another important point in Figure 7.11 is Q, which is considered to be the most visible point for the pi camera

.

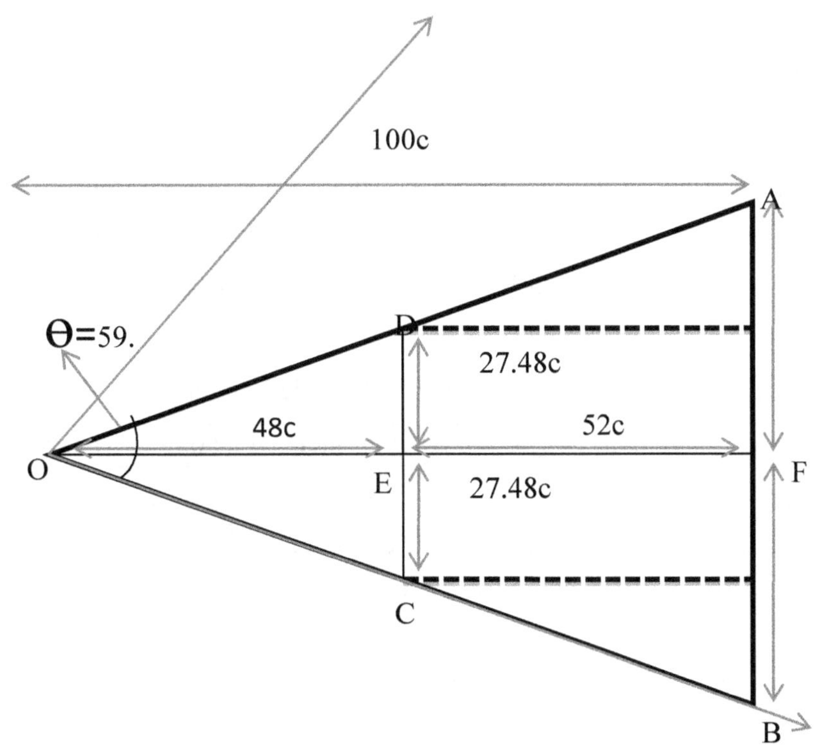

Figure 7.10 View of Raspberry pi camera.

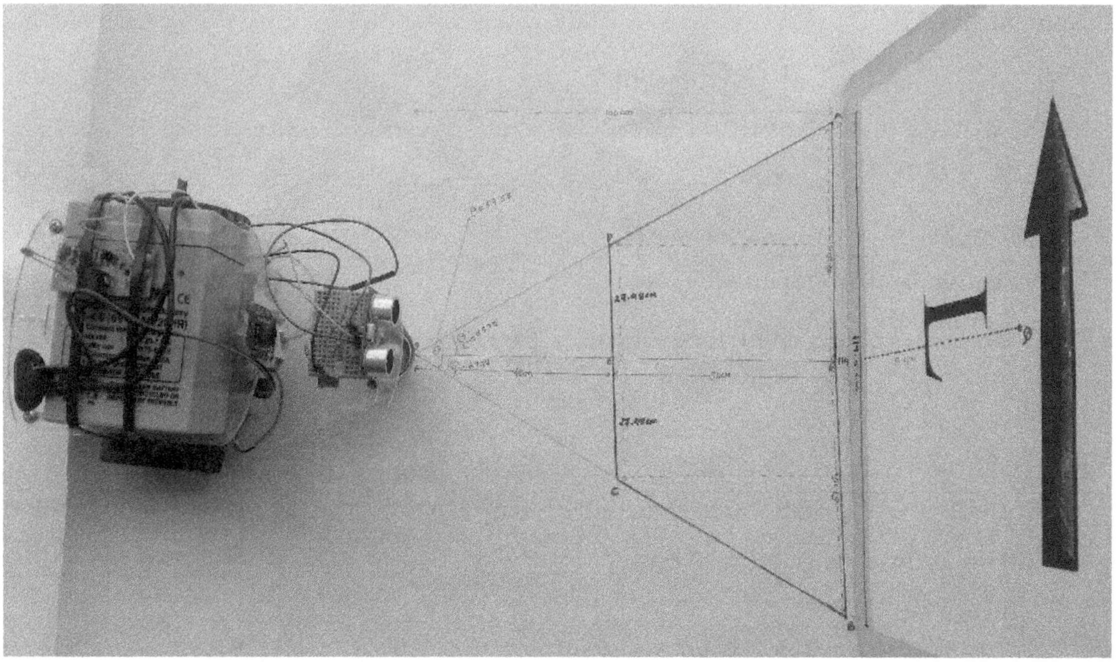

Figure 7.11 View of Image by Raspberry pi.

7.6 Average Latency Calculation

Average latency of recognizing a landmark is calculated by using GoPiGo to send the captured landmarks and the respective response (turn left for 'L', turn right for 'R', and stop for 'S') as shown in table 7.3. It is found out that the average latency is 6.4 seconds.

Table 7.3 Latency Time for Recognizing for 3 Sample Landmarks ('S', 'L', 'R').

Sl. No.	Landmark	Time taken to identify land mark (in secs)
1	'R'	7
2	'R'	6
3	'R'	8
4	'L'	5
5	'L'	6
6	'L'	7
7	'S'	8
8	'S'	6
9	'S'	5
10	'S'	6

7.7 Summary of the Chapter

The chapter provides an insight to the actual implementation of cloud enabled robotic framework using landmark and variable length string.

The test bed 3 is tested successfully and the following points are observed.

- Variable length string is generated while navigating.

- The latency time taken to communicate between cloud and robot came out to be 6.4 seconds. Hence real time navigation needs access to high bandwidth internet connection with latency.

- Therefore landmark based can be used for decision making but not suitable for real time applications.

A CLOUD COMPUTING ARCHITECTURE FOR ROBOTS

by

DHRUBA NINGOMBAM

Registration Number 201210013

DEPARTMENT OF COMPUTER SCIENCE AND ENGINEERING

SIKKIM MANIPAL INSTITUTE OF TECHNOGY

Submitted

In partial fulfillment of the requirement of the degree of

DOCTOR OF PHILOSOPHY

to the

INSPIRED BY LIFE

SMU SIKKIM MANIPAL UNIVERSITY

Established under Govt.of Sikkim, Act 9 of 1995, recognised under 2(f) of the UGC Act, 1956

August 2019

Chapter 8

Conclusion, Limitation and Future Scope

8.1 Conclusion

The literature survey reveals that robots in conjunction with cloud can become smarter and light weight and reduce the redundancy of code and data by offloading heavy processing to the cloud instead of relying on their own processors. It can put an end to a robot's capability being confined in its physical body. As cloud robotics is still in its infancy, many researches are attributed to identify the issues of communications in different robot platforms of varied hardware devices. It also points out the need for a unified and standardized data format for robot–cloud interaction.

In Chapter 3 a generic architecture is discussed wherein robots can be linked through the cloud with various communication devices. Though the concept of sharing knowledge has been proposed in the literature, the difficulties in dealing with different processors which do not support ROS or connection devices with low data transfer rate are the burning issues of the day. In the subsequent chapters, initiatives have been made to resolve these issues.

The proposed Knowledge Interchange Format (KIF) in Chapter 4 deals with the communication of heterogeneous robots on the generic architecture. Keeping in mind the size of data, emphasis has been given to generate a representation of path for robots that can be processed parallely and saved in the cloud, enabling sharing of knowledge between Robots. In order to achieve this compatibility, a path as a set of characters or a string is considered with a convention that is predefined so that no matter how much the robotics evolves, it can always interpret a string. Hadoop has been set up where paths get stored and a Map Reduce program is written to process the paths parallelly and provide the best path.

The use of high level programming API's facilitates the robots to use the processing power and machine learning models through cloud as seen in Chapter 5 and Chapter 7, whereas Chapter 6 exhibits the capability of intelligence sharing between heterogeneous robots.

For real time processing, a high bandwidth internet and devices gives better performance in terms of time taken to get the response from the cloud. With a lesser bandwidth internet and devices, shorter message format as in chapter 5 and 6 are preferred.

In Chapter 5, a cloud architecture comprising an android application middleware as an interface for communication between the cloud infrastructure and the robot has been developed for fixed length communication. Standard Application programming interface (API) has been used to harness the database and computing power of cloud. The architecture has been illustrated with a case study of Cloud-Enabled Robotic Framework for Library Assistant as Test bed – I for automatic sorting of books by robots exploiting the rich database of books from the cloud.

Since robotics evolves very fast it becomes pertinent from the economic viewpoint that whatever is implemented in the past should be compatible in the future. In order to achieve this compatibility, intelligence sharing between heterogeneous robots has been attempted in Chapter 6. Here, a map is defined as a set of characters or a string with a predefined convention that no matter how much robotics evolves, it can always interpret a string and as such this map will be useful to all. As an experimental set up with limited resources and hardware constraints, only two robots have been deployed and the network connectivity is implemented on Bluetooth. To reduce the complexity of the task, no sensors have been deployed to detect any changes in the environment after the command has been given and hence the robot may not compensate with the dynamic change in the environment. Further improvements can be made by using a wider network and better robot connectivity using efficient MAC policies like Wifi, Zigbee. By employing Android Application the Robots can also be enabled to record their paths for sharing purposes. Accordingly, this technique of intelligence sharing can be implemented on wider ranges of robot families.

Further to Chapter 5, the implementation of cloud enabled robotic framework using landmark and variable knowledge format has been developed in Chapter 7. The Raspberry Pi, the gateway of GoPiGo robot used in this experiment communicates with the cloud and acts as a medium to capture the real time images of landmarks sensed by ultrasonic sensors. It gets a response from the cloud in the form of json. This is used for GoPiGo to make a decision to navigate further and generate a path map. The path map is stored in the cloud for sharing with any other robot. The follower robot needs to localize itself relative to this map for which Markov localization is used. Calibration with respect to the difference in wheel-diameter has also been depicted. A generalized string has been considered to generate a common path understood by all the robots. To take into account the variation in the size of the wheels and the chassis of the robot, the follower robots are calibrated each time before using the map. Environmental factors like friction coefficients of the surface on which the robot is running can also cause the robot to deviate from its path and need to be explored in future.

From all the test beds, variable and fixed string proved to be more efficient in terms of time taken to communicate with the cloud. The variable length string is compatible with various kinds of robot.

Table 8.1 listed below are conclusions drawn from the experiments conducted.

Table 8.1 Fixed length String versus Variable length string

Fixed length String	Variable length String
The fixed length string could be deployed in a situation where only a single path exists between a source and a destination.	The Variable length string could be deployed in a situation where there exist multiple paths between a source and a destination.

An attempt has been made to formulate a format for representing knowledge in the form of a variable string which is compatible with all hardware of robots. This format is perfect for slow connectivity since the size of data is in terms of few kilobytes.Since robots are used extensively in this era, such sharing of code would reduce the time and effort in recoding and data required for robots which does similar tasks using cloud.

8.2 Limitations

- The proposed architecture and KIF provide satisfactory results for sharing intelligence. However, absence or slow internet connectivity increases the latency and hampers real time decision making.
- Path map is designed with an ideal environment without considering obstacles and odometry errors.
- While the framework is expected to work on all the robots, the test beds are restricted to only 3 types of robots, *viz;* a) Boe-bot b) Lego Mindstorm NXT c) GoPiGo

8.3 Future Scope

- The Knowledge interchange can be extended to store other information such as object models, information about particular environment knowledge, than a path map.

- Common tasks performed by robots such as grasping, series of movements for joints (kinematics redundancy) can also be incorporated as a high level service.

- More families of robots can be involved other than the ones used in the test bed of this thesis.

References

[1] AI cloud services. (n.d.). Retrieved May 16, 2019, from http://noosware.com/ai-cloud-services.

[2] Anders, C. (2010, December 17). Google releases Android robot libraries. Retrieved December 18, 2015, from http://diydrones.com/profiles/blogs/google-releases-android-robot .

[3] Arumugam, R., Enti, V. R., Bingbing, L., Xiaojun, W., Baskaran, K., Kong, F. F., ... & Kit, G. W. (2010, May). DAvinCi: A cloud computing framework for service robots. In *2010 IEEE international conference on robotics and automation* (pp. 3084-3089). IEEE.

[4] Bacciu, D., Gallicchio, C., Micheli, A., Di Rocco, M., &Saffiotti, A. (2014, July). Learning context-aware mobile robot navigation in home environments. In *IISA 2014, The 5th International Conference on Information, Intelligence, Systems and Applications* (pp. 57-62). IEEE.

[5] Bargar, A. (2012). A comprehensive ROS interface for the Aldebaran NAO.

[6] Beal, V. (n.d.). Mobile Operating Systems (Mobile OS) Explained. Retrieved February 12, 2019, from https://www.webopedia.com/DidYouKnow/Hardware_Software/mobile-operating-systems-mobile-os-explained.html

[7] Ben-Ari, M., & Mondada, F. (2018). Robots and their applications. In *Elements of Robotics* (pp. 1-20). Springer, Cham.

[8] Bohez, S., Verbelen, T., De Coninck, E., Vankeirsbilck, B.,

Simoens, P., & Dhoedt, B. (2017, September). Sensor fusion for robot control through deep reinforcement learning. In *2017 IEEE/RSJ International Conference on Intelligent Robots and Systems (IROS)* (pp. 2365-2370). IEEE.

[9] C2RO Cloud Robotics. (2018 August 12). Retrieved January 2, 2019, from https://www.roboticsbusinessreview.com/listing/c2ro-robotics.

[10] Capek, K. (2004), R.U.R. (Rossum's universal robots), Penguin classics. London: Penguin Books.

[11] Chen, W., Yaguchi, Y., Naruse, K., Watanobe, Y., Nakamura, K., & Ogawa, J. (2018). A study of robotic cooperation in cloud robotics: Architecture and challenges. *IEEE Access*, 6, 36662-36682.

[12] Chettri, P., Ningombam, D., Singh, C. T., & Ghose, M. K. (February 2016). An Introduction to Ontology: Survey", *IJISET - International Journal of Innovative Science, Engineering & Technology*, 3(2), 576-582.

[13] Chinchali, S., Sharma, A., Harrison, J., Elhafsi, A., Kang, D., Pergament, E., ... &Pavone, M. (2019). Network offloading policies for cloud robotics: a learning-based approach. *arXiv preprint arXiv:1902.05703*.

[14] Conroy, P. J. (2013). *The development of an aerial robotics laboratory highlighting the first experimental validation of optimal reciprocal collision avoidance*. The University of Utah.

[15] Control Boe Bot with Android Phone via Bluetooth module? (n.d.). Retrieved May 1, 2014, from

https://forums.parallax.com/discussion/131106/control-boe-bot-with-android-phone-via-bluetooth-module

[16] Corke, P. (2017). *Robotics, vision and control: fundamental algorithms in MATLAB® second, completely revised* (Vol. 118). Springer.

[17] Correll, N. "Introduction to Autonomous Robots", 1st edition, ISBN13:978-1493773077, 2014.

[18] Downes, P. (2013, May 09). How Innovations Become Better And Cheaper. Retrieved June 18, 2019, from https://www.forbes.com/sites/bigbangdisruption/2013/05/09/welcome-to-the-world-of-better-and-cheaper/.

[19] Duggan, L., Dowzard, J., Katupitiya, J., & Chan, K. C. (2017). A rapid deployment big data computing platform for cloud robotics. *International Journal of Computer Networks and Communications*, *9*(6), 77-88.

[20] Element14, F. (n.d.). Raspberry Pi. Retrieved October 10, 2016, from https://in.element14.com/buy-raspberry-pi?ost=Raspberry+Pi

[21] Elkady, A., &Sobh, T. (2012). Robotics middleware: A comprehensive literature survey and attribute-based bibliography. Journal of Robotics, 2012.

[22] Etzkorn, L. H. (2017). *Introduction to Middleware: Web Services, Object Components, and Cloud Computing*. CRC Press.

[23] Folkesson, A. (2017, September 18). Lab 2: Programming in LEGO Mindstorms NXT. Retrieved March 2, 2018, from http://www.it.uu.se/edu/course/homepage/realtid/ht16/lab2

[24] Fortino, G., Guerrieri, A., Russo, W., &Savaglio, C. (2014). Middlewares for smart objects and smart environments: overview and comparison. In *Internet of Things Based on Smart Objects* (pp. 1-27). Springer, Cham.

[25] Fox, D. (1998). *Markov localization: A probabilistic framework for mobile robot localization and navigation* (Doctoral dissertation, Verlag nicht ermittelbar).

[26] Genesereth, M. R. (n.d.). Knowledge Interchange Format. Retrieved February 14, 2013, from http://logic.stanford.edu/kif/kif.html.

[27] Gera, D. L. (2003). *Ancient Greek ideas on speech, language, and civilization.* Oxford University Press, USA.

[28] Getting Started with Stamps in Class - Parallax, Inc. (n.d.). Retrieved March 2, 2018, from https://www.parallax.com/sites/default/files/downloads/28125-Getting-Started-from-Help-v2.5.pdf .

[29] Gill, A. Q. (2015). Adaptive Cloud Enterprise Architecture: Intelligent. *Information Systems,* 4.World Scientific, page 15, June 8

[30] Goldberg, K., & Kehoe, B. (2013). Cloud robotics and automation: A survey of related work. *EECS Department, University of California, Berkeley, Tech. Rep. UCB/EECS-2013-5.*

[31] Gonzalez, N., Miers, C., Redigolo, F., Simplicio, M., Carvalho, T., Näslund, M., & Pourzandi, M. (2012). A quantitative analysis of current security concerns and solutions for cloud computing.

Journal of Cloud Computing: Advances, Systems and Applications, 1(1), 11.

[32] Hadoop Map Reduce. (n.d.). Retrieved July 23, 2017, from http://hadoop.apache.org/docs/r1.2.1/mapred_tutorial.html

[33] Hadoop, What it is and why it matters (n.d.). Retrieved October 03, 2017, from https://www.sas.com/en_us/insights/big-data/hadoop.html.

[34] Hashizume, K., Rosado, D. G., Fernández-Medina, E., & Fernandez, E. B. (2013). An analysis of security issues for cloud computing. *Journal of internet services and applications, 4*(1), 5.

[35] Hayet, J. B., Lerasle, F., &Devy, M. (2002, May). A visual landmark framework for indoor mobile robot navigation. In *Proceedings 2002 IEEE International Conference on Robotics and Automation (Cat. No. 02CH37292)* (Vol. 4, pp. 3942-3947). IEEE.

[36] HDFS Architecture. (n.d.). Retrieved May 8, 2018, from https://hadoop.apache.org/docs/current/hadoop-project-dist/hadoop-hdfs/HdfsDesign.html

[37] History of Robotics: Timeline. (n.d.). Retrieved February 18, 2019, from https://www.robotshop.com/media/files/PDF/timeline.pdf

[38] Hong, J. H., Min, B. C., Taylor, J. M., Raskin, V., & Matson, E. T. (2012, October). NL-based communication with firefighting robots. In *2012 IEEE International Conference on Systems, Man, and Cybernetics (SMC)* (pp. 1461-1466). IEEE.

[39] Horne, M., Niobe, Nick, Chris, Haight, D., Lance, . . . Dimas. (2014, July 22). Ultrasonic Distance Measurement Using Python –

Part 2. Retrieved October 10, 2018, from https://www.raspberrypi-spy.co.uk/2013/01/ultrasonic-distance-measurement-using-python-part-2/

[40] Hossain, A., & Shirazi, F. (2015, August). Cloud Computing: A Multi-tenant Case Study. *In International Conference on Human-Computer Interaction* (pp. 178-189). Springer, Cham.

[41] Hosseini, S. H., &Goher, K. M. (2016). Personal care robots for older adults: An overview. Asian Social Science, 13(1), 11–19.

[42] How Robots Could Help the Elderly Age in Their Homes. (2017, August 29). Retrieved January 2, 2018, from https://www.smithsonianmag.com/innovation/how-robots-could-help-elderly-age-in-their-homes-180964650/.

[43] How to Connect to a Raspberry Pi Directly with an Ethernet Cable. (2017, July 12). Retrieved October 3, 2017, from https://www.circuitbasics.com/how-to-connect-to-a-raspberry-pi-directly-with-an-ethernet-cable.

[44] How to: Boe-Bot Robot with Easy Bluetooth Module [Video file]. (2009, May 11). Retrieved November 21, 2014, from https://www.youtube.com/watch?v=Y1W0gm5nyoca.

[45] Hu, G., Tay, W. P., & Wen, Y. (2012). Cloud robotics: architecture, challenges and applications. *IEEE network, 26*(3), 21-28.

[46] Ibrahim, A., Alexander, R. R., Sanghar, M. S. U., & D'Souza, R. D. (2016). Control Systems in Robotics: A Review. *International Journal of Engineering Inventions, 5*(5), 29-38.

[47] III, F. (2019, March 02). The Main Parts of a Robot. Retrieved April 13, 2019, from https://sciencing.com/main-parts-robot-7403157.html

[48] Inaba, M. (1997, August). Remote-brained robots. In *IJCAI* (pp. 1593-1606).

[49] Industrial robot sales increase worldwide by 31 percent, International Federation of Robotics, Press Releases, Munich, Jun 20, 2018.

[50] Jordan, S., Haidegger, T., Kovács, L., Felde, I., & Rudas, I. (2013, July). The rising prospects of cloud robotic applications. In *2013 IEEE 9th International Conference on Computational Cybernetics (ICCC)* (pp. 327-332). IEEE.

[51] Kalashnikov, A., Zhang, H., Jennings, J., &Abramriuk, M. M. (2017). Remote laboratory: using Internet-of-Things (IoT) for E-learning.

[52] Kehoe, B., Matsukawa, A., Candido, S., Kuffner, J., & Goldberg, K. (2013, May). Cloud-based robot grasping with the google object recognition engine. In *2013 IEEE International Conference on Robotics and Automation* (pp. 4263-4270). IEEE.

[53] Kehoe, B., Patil, S., Abbeel, P., & Goldberg, K. (2015). A survey of research on cloud robotics and automation. *IEEE Transactions on automation science and engineering, 12*(2), 398-409.

[54] Kerl, C., Sturm, J., &Cremers, D. (2013, May). Robust odometry estimation for RGB-D cameras. In *2013 IEEE International Conference on Robotics and Automation* (pp. 3748-3754). IEEE.

[55] Kharel, A., Bhutia, D., Rai, S., &Ningombam, D. (2014). Cloud robotics using ROS. *International Journal of Computer Applications*, 18-21.

[56] King, D. (2001, June). Space servicing: past, present and future. In *Proceedings of the 6th International Symposium on Artificial Intelligence and Robotics & Automation in Space: i-SAIRAS* (pp. 18-22).

[57] Kulkarni, G., Khatawkar, P., & Gambhir, J. (2011). Cloud computing-platform as service. *International Journal of Engineering, 1*.

[58] Kulkarni, G., Shelke, R., Palwe, R., Solanke, V., Belsare, S., & Mohite, S. (2014, April). Mobile cloud computing-bring your own device. In *2014 Fourth International Conference on Communication Systems and Network Technologies* (pp. 565-568). IEEE.

[59] Kulkarni, G., Sutar, R. & Gambhir, J., 2012. Cloud Computing-Infrastructure as Service - Amazon EC2. *International Journal of Engineering Research and Applications, 2*(1), pp. 117-125.

[60] Kulkarni,G. (2012). Cloud computing-software as service. International Journal of Cloud Computing And Services Science, 1(1), 11.

[61] Kumar, S. V. K., &Padmapriya, S. (2014). A survey on cloud computing security threats and vulnerabilities. *International Journal Innovative Research in Electrical, Electronics, Instrumentation and control Engineering*, ISSN (Online)-2321-2004.

[62] Lai, K., & Fox, D. (2010). Object recognition in 3D point clouds

using web data and domain adaptation. *The International Journal of Robotics Research, 29*(8), 1019-1037.

[63] Lee, S. J., Lim, J., Tewolde, G., & Kwon, J. (2014, June). Autonomous tour guide robot by using ultrasonic range sensors and QR code recognition in indoor environment. In *IEEE International Conference on Electro/Information Technology* (pp. 410-415). IEEE.

[64] Leiner, B. M., Cerf, V. G., Clark, D. D., Kahn, R. E., Kleinrock, L., Lynch, D. C., ... & Wolff, S. (2009). A brief history of the Internet. *ACM SIGCOMM Computer Communication Review, 39*(5), 22-31.

[65] Liljeback, P., Stavdahl, O., &Beitnes, A. (2006, December). SnakeFighter-development of a water hydraulic fire fighting snake robot. In *2006 9th International Conference on Control, Automation, Robotics and Vision* (pp. 1-6). IEEE.

[66] Lim, J. H., Song, S. H., Kuc, T. Y., Park, H. S., & Kim, H. S. (2009, December). A hierarchical test model and automated test framework for RTC. In *International Conference on Future Generation Information Technology* (pp. 198-207). Springer, Berlin, Heidelberg.

[67] Limosani, R., Manzi, A., Fiorini, L., Cavallo, F., & Dario, P. (2016). Enabling global robot navigation based on a cloud robotics approach. *International Journal of Social Robotics, 8*(3), 371-380.

[68] Lindhorst, T., &Nett, E. (2015). Dependable communication for mobile robots in industrial wireless mesh networks. In *Cooperative Robots and Sensor Networks 2015* (pp. 207-227). Springer, Cham.

[69] Loughlin, C. (2010). Deep water robots. Industrial Robot: *An International Journal.*

[70] Maimone, M., Biesiadecki, J., Tunstel, E., Cheng, Y., & Leger, C. (2006). Surface navigation and mobility intelligence on the Mars Exploration Rovers, Intelligence for Space Robotics.

[71] Majakorpi, M. (2013). Theory and practice of rapid elasticity in cloud applications.

[72] Manyika, J. (2017). A future that works: AI, automation, employment, and productivity. *McKinsey Global Institute Research, Tech. Rep, 60.*

[73] Marjovi, A., Choobdar, S., & Marques, L. (2012). Robotic clusters: Multi-robot systems as computer clusters: A topological map merging demonstration. *Robotics and Autonomous Systems, 60*(9), 1191-1204.

[74] Marranzino, A. (2017, May 16). Ocean Tech: Using Robots to Conduct Deep-Sea Research. Retrieved June 17, 2018, from https://oceanbites.org/ocean-tech-using-robots-to-conduct-deep-sea-research/

[75] Mell, P., &Grance, T. National Institute of Standards and Technology, US Department of Commerce, The NIST Definition of Cloud Computing, Special Publication 800-145, September 2011.

[76] Miller, A. T., & Allen, P. K. (2004). Graspit! a versatile simulator for robotic grasping. *IEEE Robotics & Automation Magazine, 11*(4), 110-122.

[77] Misra, D. K., Sung, J., Lee, K., & Saxena, A. (2016). Tell me dave: Context-sensitive grounding of natural language to manipulation instructions. *The International Journal of Robotics Research, 35*(1-3), 281-300.

[78] Mobile robots for Industry 4.0. (n.d.). Retrieved May 18, 2019 from https://aethon.com/mobile-robots-for-manufacturing.

[79] Mohamed, N., Al-Jaroodi, J., &Jawhar, I. (2008, September). Middleware for robotics: A survey. In *2008 IEEE Conference on Robotics, Automation and Mechatronics* (pp. 736-742). IEEE

[80] Mohanarajah, G., Hunziker, D., D'Andrea, R. & Waibel, M.(2015, April) "Rapyuta: A Cloud Robotics Platform," in *IEEE Transactions on Automation Science and Engineering,* vol. 12, no. 2, pp. 481-493.

[81] Nasa. (2017, July 21). The Past, Present and Future of Exploration on Mars. Retrieved March 12, 2018, from https://nasa.tumblr.com/post/163250150894/the-past-present-and-future-of-exploration-on.

[82] Oros, N., &Krichmar, J. L. (2013). Android™ Based Robotics: Powerful, Flexible and Inexpensive Robots for Hobbyists, Educators, Students and Researchers. *Cognitive Anteater Robotics Laboratory. University of California, Irvine.*

[83] Ort, T. (2013). *Art and Life in Modernist Prague: Karel Čapek and His Generation, 1911-1938*. Springer.

[84] Padhy, R. P., & Patra, M. R. (2012). Evolution of cloud computing and enabling technologies. *International Journal of Cloud Computing and Services Science, 1*(4), 182.

[85] Pandey, A. & Pooja, (2013). Cloud Computing - An on Demand Service Platform. *International Journal of Computer Applications*, 5-9.

[86] Patel, K. K., & Patel, S. M. (2016). Internet of things-IOT: definition, characteristics, architecture, enabling technologies, application & future challenges. *International journal of engineering science and computing, 6*(5).

[87] Porkodi, R., & Bhuvaneswari, V. (2014, March). The internet of things (IOT) applications and communication enabling technology standards: An overview. In *2014 International conference on intelligent computing applications* (pp. 324-329). IEEE.

[88] Prassler, E., Bischoff, R., Roboter, K. U. K. A., Bruyninckx, H., & Leuven, K. U. (2010). It's a Long Way to Useful Standards [Industrial Activities]. *IEEE Robotics & Automation Magazine, 17*(3), 18-19.

[89] Rashid, A., & Chaturvedi, A. (2017). A Study on Resource Pooling, Allocation and Virtualization Tools used for Cloud Computing. *International Journal of Computer Applications, 168*(2).

[90] Riazuelo, L., Civera, J., & Montiel, J. M. (2014). C2tam: A cloud framework for cooperative tracking and mapping. *Robotics and Autonomous Systems, 62*(4), 401-413.

[91] Robot operating system, Willow Garage, (n.d). Retrieved May 18, 2019, from http://www.willowgarage.com/pages/software/ros-platform.

[92] Robot Operating System. (n.d.). Retrieved August 18, 2014, from https://www.ros.org/.

[93] Robot Sourcing and Rules for Selfies : The Moments That Stood Out at SXSW (n.d). Retrieved January 13, 2014, from http://blogs.wsj.com/digits/2014/03/11/robot-sourcing-and-rules-for-selfies-the-moments-that-stood-out-at-sw/tab/print/?KEYWORDS=SXSW.

[94] Robots using ROS: Aldebaran Nao (n.d.). Retrieved April 18, 2010 from http://www.ros.org/news/2010/03/robots-using-ros-aldebaran-nao.html.

[95] Rosjava : An implementation of ROS in pure Java with Android support. (n.d.). Retrieved August 17, 2014, from https://github.com/rosjava.

[96] Saha, O., & Dasgupta, P. (2018). A comprehensive survey of recent trends in cloud robotics architectures and applications. *Robotics, 7*(3), 47.

[97] Schlenoff, C., Foufou, S., &Balakirsky, S. (2012, March). Performance evaluation of robotic knowledge representation (PERK). In *Proceedings of the Workshop on Performance Metrics for Intelligent Systems* (pp. 1-8).

[98] Schlenoff, C., Prestes, E., Gonçalves, P. S., Abel, M., Amirat, Y., Balakirsky, S., ... & Gérard, S. (2015). *IEEE standard ontologies for robotics and automation.*

[99] Schöllig, A., Alonso-Mora, J., &D'Andrea, R. (2013). Limited benefit of joint estimation in multi-agent iterative learning control. *Asian J. Control (Special Issue on Iterative Learning Control),*

15(4), 1-11.

[100] SecaaS Implementation Guidance: Catego,y 1 Identity and Access Management. (n.d.). Retrieved September 4, 2016, from https://cloudsecurityalliance.org.

[101] Siegwart, R., Nourbakhsh, I. R., &Scaramuzza, D. (2011). *Introduction to autonomous mobile robots*. MIT press.

[102] Siewert, S. (2012). Cloud-based education, Part 3: Cloud-based robotics for education.

[103] Simoens, P., Dragone, M., &Saffiotti, A. (2018). The Internet of Robotic Things: A review of concept, added value and applications. *International Journal of Advanced Robotic Systems, 15*(1), 1729881418759424.

[104] Slack, M. G. (1993, April). Autonomous navigation of mobile robots for real-world applications. In *21st AIPR Workshop on Interdisciplinary Computer Vision: An Exploration of Diverse Applications* (Vol. 1838, pp. 101-109). International Society for Optics and Photonics.

[105] Smart, W. D. (2007, October). Is a common middleware for robotics possible?. In *Proceedings of the IROS 2007 workshop on Measures and Procedures for the Evaluation of Robot Architectures and Middleware. Citeseer* (Vol. 1).

[106] Space Robots. (n.d.). Retrieved March 7, 2019, from https://spectrum.ieee.org/robotics/space-robots.

[107] Srinivas, J., Reddy, K. V. S., & Qyser, A. M. (2012). Cloud computing basics. *International journal of advanced research in computer and communication engineering, 1*(5), 343-347.

[108] Staranowicz, A., & Mariottini, G. L. (2011, May). A survey and comparison of commercial and open-source robotic simulator software. In *Proceedings of the 4th International Conference on PErvasive Technologies Related to Assistive Environments* (pp. 1-8).

[109] Tabassam, S. (2017). Security and privacy issues in cloud computing environment. *Journal of Information Technology & Software Engineering.*

[110] Tan, C. F., Liew, S. M., Alkahari, M. R., Ranjit, S. S. S., Said, M. R., Chen, W., & Sivakumar, D. (2013). Firefighting mobile robot: state of the art and recent development.

[111] The brain of GoPiGo board. (n.d.). Retrieved October 10 2018, from http://www.gadgetexplained.com/gadget.

[112] The Red Sea Robotic Exploratorium, Enabling Intuitive Underwater Telemanipulation. (n.d.). Retrieved April 11, 2019, from https://cs.stanford.edu/group/manips/projects/redsearobotics.html.

[113] Using Cellphones as Robotic Control Platforms. (n.d.). Retrieved November 21, 2015, from http://www.cellbots.com/software/java.

[114] Waher, P. (2015). *Learning internet of things.* Packt Publishing Ltd.

[115] Waibel, M., Beetz, M., Civera, J., d'Andrea, R., Elfring, J., Galvez-Lopez, D., ... & Schiessle, B. (2011). Roboearth. *IEEE Robotics & Automation Magazine, 18*(2), 69-82.

[116] Wan, J., Tang, S., Yan, H., Li, D., Wang, S., &Vasilakos, A. V. (2016). Cloud robotics: Current status and open issues. *IEEE Access, 4, 2797-2807.*

[117] Wang, L., Liu, M., & Meng, M. Q. H. (2015). Real-time multisensor data retrieval for cloud robotic systems. *IEEE Transactions on Automation Science and Engineering, 12*(2), 507-518.

[118] Whelan, T., Johannsson, H., Kaess, M., Leonard, J. J., & McDonald, J. (2013, May). Robust real-time visual odometry for dense RGB-D mapping. In *2013 IEEE International Conference on Robotics and Automation* (pp. 5724-5731). IEEE.

[119] Wiener, P. (2016, September 09). This Robot Could Make Exploring Oceans Deeper, Faster, and Cheaper. Retrieved May 11, 2019, from https://www.nationalgeographic.com/adventure/features/underwater-robot-submarine/

[120] Zadka, G. M., & Lefkowitz, G. (2010). The twisted network framework.

[121] Zainuddin, N. A., Mustafah, Y. M., Shawgi, Y. A. M., & Rashid, N. K. A. M. (2014, September). Autonomous navigation of mobile robot using Kinect sensor. In *2014 International Conference on Computer and Communication Engineering* (pp. 28-31). IEEE.

[122] Zhang, Q., Cheng, L., &Boutaba, R. (2010). Cloud computing: state-of-the-art and research challenges. *Journal of internet services and applications, 1*(1), 7-18.

[123] Zhang, S., Sun, L., Dong, L., Yuan, B., Chen, Z., & Liu, J. (2014,

July). Initial location calibration of home service robot based on 2-dimensional codes landmarks. In *Proceedings of the 33rd Chinese Control Conference* (pp. 8315-8320). IEEE.

[124] Zhu, J. (2010). Cloud computing technologies and applications. In *Handbook of cloud computing* (pp. 21-45). Springer, Boston, MA.

[125] Zissis, D., & Lekkas, D. (2012). Addressing cloud computing security issues. *Future Generation computer systems, 28*(3), 583-592.

[126] ZXing ("Zebra Crossing") barcode scanning library for Java, Android. (n.d.). Retrieved August 21, 2020, from https://opensource.google.com/projects/zxing.

www.ingramcontent.com/pod-product-compliance
Lightning Source LLC
LaVergne TN
LVHW082351200926
848481LV00012B/3532
* 9 7 9 8 2 3 2 6 9 9 0 9 3 *